I0166473

Porter Sermon Outlines

by W. Curtis Porter

Published by Guardian of Truth Foundation

ISBN 1-58427-060-8

Guardian of Truth Foundation
P.O. Box 9670
Bowling Green, Kentucky 42102

Introduction

It is a genuine pleasure to me to be able to present this most useful volume of sermon outlines by the late W. Curtis Porter. These outlines have been tested through the years and proven true to the word of God. They have been used in causing many to learn the truth and obey it; they have taught many the differences between truth and error within the church and outside it.

These outlines cover many subjects with a wide range of study. They will beneficially serve the preachers who will wisely use them. As one can quickly observe they are full of Book, Chapter, and Verse citations. This was the kind of preaching by brother Porter himself, and was thrilled in his presentation of the Old Story.

Brother Porter has now been gone from us for more than twenty years, but his work of labor remains, and we send it forth with expectation to accomplish good.

----- Earl E. Robertson

W. Curtis Porter
1897-1960

William Curtis Porter
A Biographical Sketch

Paul C. Keller

William Curtis Porter, the second son of Benjamin and Laura Privett Porter, was born at Myrtle, Miss., on February 26, 1897. In 1898 the Porter family moved to Arkansas, moving first to the Mangrum community in eastern Craighead County. Later they moved near what was then Obear for three years. During this time, Curtis, at the age of four, attended his first term of school at Weiner.

From Obear the family returned to the Mangrum community and settled permanently. Eastern Craighead County was then largely unsettled and undeveloped. The land was fertile but clearing and cultivating it was hard work. Early in life Curtis learned to work hard, a trait which characterized him throughout life.

Religious feelings ran high in the area. Settlers coming from other states brought with them their religious convictions and prejudices. In the Mangrum community was a congregation of disciples. Here the Porters heard the pure gospel of Christ and obeyed it. At the age of fourteen, Curtis was baptized by Jesse T. Lashlee, in July of 1911.

His formal education was received in the public schools of Arkansas and one year was spent at Old Monea College at Rector, Ark. Although his formal education was limited he was, by this own self-application, a well-educated man. He never quit studying, but was a diligent and systematic student as long as he lived.

Brother Porter married Miss Jessie Winstead in April of 1917, when he was twenty years of age, and for more than thirty-seven years they met the challenges of life together. She was a devoted Christian and was ever a source of help and encouragement to her beloved husband. No children were born of this union. A motherless niece, Melba Taylor, was reared and educated by the Porters. Death came for Jessie in January of 1955.

His Preaching

Brother Porter began his preaching career in 1914 at Mangrum, at the age of seventeen. For the next few years he was kept busy preaching at his home congregation and other places near his home. In 1923 he moved to Springfield, Mo., to work full time with the Johnson and Dale congregation. In the years that followed he worked with congregations in Wichita, Kan., Weatherford, Texas, Sacramento, Calif., and Tusla, Okla., until 1942. From 1917 until his death he held several meetings per year, preaching in most of the states.

He was an able preacher. His lessons were always well prepared, logical and scriptural, and were forcefully delivered.

His Writings

Through the years brother Porter wrote for various religious papers. He contributed frequent articles to the *Christian Worker*, *Firm Foundation*, *Bible Banner*, *Gospel Advocate* and others. He was one of the original Associate Editors of the *Gospel Guardian*, serving in this capacity until his death. He wrote many poems which were published in various magazines and papers. He was the author of various tracts and booklets, including: "Divine Healing," "Dissolving A Few Baptist Asprins," and "Ask Your Precher."

His Debating

Perhaps the name of W. Curtis Porter is best know for his work on the polemic platform. Through the years he was recognized as one of the ablest defenders of the faith to be found anywhere. He engaged in his first debate when he was eighteen years old, meeting D.N. Jackson, Baptist, at the old Kentucky settlement (now Hancock), a few miles from his boyhood home. He acquitted himself well, and any uneasiness brethren felt because of his age and inexperience was quickley allayed. He proved to be master of the situation from first to last, and the brethren were elated with his able defense of the truth. In years to follow he met Jackson in six other debates, more times than he met any other man.

He participated in seventy-seven debates, meeting representative men of many different religious bodies on a great variety of subjects. He was truly outstanding as a debater. He was fair and courteous in his treatment of every opponent, but was methodical and unrelenting in exposing his errors. In a masterful way he unmasked sophistry and made an opponent's quibbles "backfire." He had the agility of mind to immediately detect the fallacy of an argument and the ability to expose the fallacy to the discomfort of its advocate and the chagrin of his supporters.

From various parts of the nation brethren called him to defend the truth against many false doctrines. They felt confident that W. Curtis Porter would do the job well. They were never disappointed. As a debater we have never heard his superior. His equal would be hard to find.

These oral debates are in book form; Porter-Tingley, Porter-Bogard, Porter-Waters, and Porter-Woods. Two written debates are in book form: Porter-Dugger and Porter-Myers.

Blood Malady

For the last eighteen years of life brother Porter's work was greatly hampered by ill-health. In 1942 he was stricken with Polycythemia vera, a rare blood disease, usually fatal within two years. Being advised that his life expectancy would be from two to four years, he resigned his work with the Tenth and Rockford church, Tulsa, Okla., and moved back to his home area, Monette, Ark. He continued a busy schedule of preaching, writing and debating. The church at Monette two Sundays per month. Through his efforts a good-sized congregation was built up and a building erected and paid for.

In the meantime his blood malady was gradually taking its toll. In 1944, when death seemed imminent, he learned of experimental treatments being given by a California doctor. While the nature of the treatment was then a secret, one of the men who helped develop atomic energy was using atomic isotopes to treat Polycythemia. Brother Porter was accepted for treatments and while these did not prove fully successful they did result in his life being prolonged for another sixteen years of service.

During these years he engaged in many significant debates, more than half his debated occurring during this period. He continued to preach at various places near his home and conducted several meetings each year. During the last few years of his life he preached for the Ninth and Hafford church, Rector, Ark., the Harrison Street church, Kennett, Mo., and the church at Caraway, Ark., near his boyhood home.

Brother Porter married Mrs. Mary McGowan, December 26,

1955. Mary, a devoted Christian and faithful wife, was a source of help and encouragement. Her devoted attention to him and her constant solicitude for his welfare contributed much to his happiness and usefulness to the very close of his life. Remembrance of these years of love, labor, sacrifice and accomplishment must be a source of satisifaction and comfort to sister Porter in these hours of bereavement and lonliness.

From 1942 to the close of his life brother Porter was hindered by a continuing series of physical difficulties. His blook malady weakened his resistance and made him a prey to many other physical disorders. He preached, debated and worked under great handicaps — worked when he was physically unable to do so, preached and debated under the stress of physical pain. Nevertheless, he always did his job well, and few knew of the handicaps under which he labored. Through it all he continued to be patient, uncomplaining and optimistic.

His Death

A short time before his death his blood malady reversed itself and he became a victim of acute leukemia. Frequent blood transfusions became necessary. He continued to work to the very end. His last meeting was with the Spring and Blaine church in St. Louis, May 8-15. Unable to complete the meeting, he was admitted to a hospital for blood transfusions. Somewhat strengthened, he returned home. During the latter part of June he entered the Baptist Hospital in Memphis, suffering with cellulitis and a sinus infection. Hemorrhaging of the sinus area and other parts of the body signalled that the end was near. He knew that a cerebral hemorrhage might occur at any time, and was unperturbed. On Monday night, July 4, he observed that such was occurring. He talked calmly with sister Porter about the approaching end, made known his wishes concerning those who were to conduct his funeral, the place for the funeral, etc. He was conscious through the night and slept early the next morning, after having been given a sedative. On the afternoon of July 5, at 2:15, the end came.

His Funeral

Funeral services were conducted July 7, at Monette, by Eugene Britnell, Edgar J. Dye, and Paul C. Keller. The church building at Monette was not large enough to accomodate the throng of neighbors and brethren from many places who gathered to pay a tribute of respect. Brethren from Caraway, where he had preached for many years and where he was appreciated and tenderly loved by all, served as active pall bearers. These were: Gordon

Graddy; Oscar Williams, Ferrel Tucker, Lexa Johnson, James Frayser and Thurmond Miller. Honorary pall bearers were: W.K. Wallace, Joe McInturff, Franklin T. Puckett, H.S. Owens, James L. Gay, H.F. Sharp, Cleo Blue, Jesse-Kelley and James L. Yopp. His body was laid to rest in the Monette Cemetery.

In addition to his wife, he is survived by three brothers, Kyle of Black Oak, Ark., E. Lacy of Benton, Ill., and Reuben of Wilmington, Calif., and by several nieces and nephews.

His Influence

It is not the purpose of this article to appraise the work and influence of W. Curtis Porter. Much could be said. We are not equal to the task. his memory is deserving of honor. His life of service merits the gratitude of brethren everywhere. Knowing that his life of purity, consecration and faithfulness has said more in its deeds than we can every say in words, we close by calling to mind two utterances of David: "Know ye not that there is a prince and a great man fallen this day in Israel?" "Tell it not in Gath, publish it not in the streets of Ashkelon; lest the daughters of the Philistines rejoice, lest the daughters of the uncircumcised triumph."

Table Of Contents

How To Study The Bible
2 Tim. 2:15

I. **Introduction.**
   A. Importance of Bible Study.
      1. Our only means of knowing God, Christ, heaven or hell.
      2. Our only source of spiritual light. Psa. 119:105, 130.
      3. If ignorant of Bible, in darkness, regardless of other attainments. Why?
      4. The basis of all faith (Rom. 10:17) ground of all hope. (Rom. 15:4)
   B. Why some read it a life-time and know little about it.

II. **Discussion.**
   A. Methods of Bible stu ly.
      1. Fall open at random - nothing definite in view.
         a. Ill.: Man opened at book of Jonah.
         b. May open today at Joseph, son of Jacob; tomorrow at Joseph husband of Mary; next day at Joseph of Arimathea - mixed.
         c. Open today at Saul seeking to kill David; tomorrow at Saul persecuting church - Sauls mixed.
      2. Book by book - from "lid to lid."
         a. Order of books arranged by man - not order of occurrence.
         b. Read return of Israel from captivity (Ezra and Nehemiah) before their going into captivity. (Ezekiel and Daniel.)
      3. The analytical method.
         a. First a general view - bird's eye view of it.
         b. Ill.: Studying map in Geography.
         c. Ill.: On Capitol building at Topeka.
         d. Two Testaments - Three dispensations - two divisions, subdivisions.
   B. Rules for Bible Study.
      1. Note the speaker - whether God or devil, etc.

1

        a. Devil is liar and father of it. John 8:44.
           (1) Examples: To Eve - Old prophet 1 Kings 13.
           (2) Believe what Devil says only when he agrees
               with God.

  2. To whom addressed - not all directly applicable to
     us.
        a. Some think "our duty plain and simple we find
          on every page."
        b. Many commands not intended for us to obey.
           (1) Noah's command to build the ark. Gen. 6.
           (2) Jonah's command to preach to Nineveh.
           (3) Command requiring all males to assemble in
               Jerusalem three times a year - feast of
               Passover, feast of Pentecost, feast of Taber-
               nacles.
           (4) Command to kill those violating certain
               laws.

  3. Study each passage in its proper setting.
        a. Don't give it a meaning not intended.
        b. On prohibition - "touch not" - Col. 2:21.
        c. Funeral Sermon - "Thou shalt know hereafter."
          John 13:7.
        d. On call to preach - "No man taketh this honor."
          Heb. 5:4.
        e. Future recognition - "Thru a glass darkly." 1 Cor.
          13:12.
        f. Perceiving Heaven - "Eye hath not seen." 1 Cor.
          2:9, 10.

  4. Let Bible speak fully and freely on every subject.
        a. Every passage tells the truth but not all the truth
          on a subject.
        b. To select one passage and refuse others is unfair
          to Bible.
        c. Ill.: Juror refusing to hear but one witness.
        d. Make application to faith (Rom. 5:1; Jas. 2:24.)
          Repentance (Luke 13:3; Acts 11:18.)

  5. Approach Bible with open and honest heart.
        a. Usually find what we are looking for.
        b. Man who has mind already made up not fit for
          juror.
        c. Balaam cursing Israel (Num. 22) "Lord's anger
          was kindled against him because he went."

III. Conclusion.

A. "Search the Scriptures." Jno. 5:39.

B. Imitate the Bereans. Acts 17:10-11.

C. Always investigate before deciding.

The New Birth
Jno. 3:1-8

I. **Introduction.**
   A. Christ's favorite way of teaching - figures and parables.
   B. Plan of salvation presented in figure of birth.
   C. Chart:

WORLD	KINGDOM	ETERNAL
Birth	Birth of	Birth
.	GOD	KINGDOM

   1. Born into each to enjoy the blessings - natural, spiritual, eternal.
   D. Why come by night? "fear of Jews" - "avoid multitude" etc.
   1. Differ over things not revealed - cf. "Jesus wrote on ground."

II. **Discussion:**
   A. Importance of New Birth.
   1. No entrance into kingdom otherwise - forever lost.
   2. Can surely be understood.
   B. Meaning Of "Born of Water."
   1. Some say "natural Birth" - Nicodemus had same view. vs. 36.
   2. Others say "water" means "Spirit" - "born of water, even the Spirit."
   3. Nearly all say "water" is figurative language.
      a. Two classes of metaphors.
         (1) Those whose meaning is clear - "fox" Luke 13:31, 32.

4

(2) Those that require an added explanation -
"rivers of living water." Jno. 7:38-39.
(3) Water of Jno. 3:5 belongs to neither.
4. "Born from above" - cf. "John's baptism from
heaven." Luke 20:3-8.
C. Before kingdom established Jesus taught by figures
and parables - afterward's plain commands.
D. What Constitutes A Birth?
1. A begetting - cf. Jas. 1:18; 1 Cor. 4:15.
a. Born of water - brought forth from water.
b. How born of spoonful of water - sprinkling?
c. Water present in only one act concerning
kingdom - immersion.
d. How immersion both birth and resurrection? Cf.
Christ "first born from dead." Col. 1:18.
E. Birth of Spirit No Mystery - Explain vs. 8.
F. New Birth Explained by Example.
1. Peter addressed brethren in Pontus, Cappadocia &
Asia. 1 Pet. 1:1.
2. Had been "begotten again" vs. 2 and "born again."
vs. 23.
3. Same people assembled at Jerusalem. Acts 2:9-11.
4. Show how they were saved. Acts 2:29-41.

III. Conclusion:
A. Born of God by believing (1 Jno. 5:1), loving (1 Jno.
4:7), and doing righteousness (1 Jno. 2:29).
B. Different expressions may mean same thing.
1. Hat at cost = Converted. Matt. 18:3
2. Reduced Price = Born Again. Jno. 3:5
3. For $5.00 = Repent and be baptized. Acts 2:38

Instrumental Music

I. **Introduction.**
   A. Music loved by all classes.
      1. Nothing but kindest feeling for music.
      2. My position not a popular one. Cf. Luke 16:15.
      3. Popularity and preferences should be laid aside.
      4. Our motto: "Where Bible speaks", etc.
      5. If authorized, must use it; if not, dare not do so.

II. **Discussion.**
   A. Logical Arguments From Bible Statements.
      1. Not go beyond things written. 1 Cor. 4:6 - R.V.
      2. Not of faith - sin. Rom. 14:23.
      3. Not preach another gospel. Gal. 1:8, 9.
      4. Spirit guided into all truth. Jno. 16:13.
      5. Scriptures furnish to all good works. 2 Tim. 3:16.
      6. All things that pertain to life and godliness. 2 Pet. 1:3.
      7. Observe Christ's commandments. Mt. 28:20.
      8. Righteousness revealed through gospel. Rom. 1:17.
      9. Adding to God's Word. Rev. 22:18.
      10. Causes Division. Rom. 16:17; Jno. 17:20, 21.
      11. Must act by authority of Christ. Col. 3:17.
   B. Arguments Used to Justify It - Refuted.
      1. "David used it." Psa. 150. Also dance.
         a. David used incense, animal sacrifice, etc.
      2. "There'll be harps in heaven." Rev. 14:2.
         a. And other things not found in the church.
         b. Cf. "As." R.V.
      3. Doesn't say, "Thou shalt not have organ."
         a. Neither "Thou shalt not bring cackling hen."
         b. Cfa. Ps. 150:6.
      4. "Can see no harm." Cf. Cain and Ussah.
      5. "If right in home, right in church."
         a. Church of Corinth thought that about eating.
      6. "Psallo involves instruments." Cf. *Baptidzo* - instru-

6

ment and element involved - but kind must be specified.

C. Wrong to Do As Religious Worship Anything Not Commanded. Lev. 10:1-3.

D. Things Right Within Themselves But Wrong Religiously.
   1. Washing pots. cups, etc. Mark. 7:1-9
   2. Eating meat - wrong with Lord's supper.
   3. Instrumental music.

E. Examples of Singing and Admonitions.
   1. Sang a hymn. Mt. 26:30
   2. Paul and Silas. Acts 16:25
   3. Sing with spirit. 1 Cor. 14:15
   4. Is any merry? - sing. Jas. 5:13

F. Scope of Divine Commandment Enjoining Music. 5:19; Col. 3:16.

CHART

ARK — Gen. 6
Wood

Oak	Elm	Gopher
Red - Black White	Red - Slippery	

Water of Separation — Num. 19
Animal

Horses	Sheep	Goats	Cattle
Black Bay	Black White	Black White	Oxen Heifer
			Black
			Red

Worship
Music

Instrumental		Vocal	
Psaltery	Harp	Soprano	Alto
Cymbals	Trimbrels	Tenor	Bass
Guitar	Violen	Baritone	
Organ	Horn		

III. **Conclusion.**
   A. We should strive for consistency.
   B. Truth is always consistent.

Baptism

I. **Introduction.**
   A. Subject engaged attention of wisest men.
   B. If any subject exhausted - this is it.
   C. As important today as ever.
   D. Lay aside preconceived ideas - study as though uninspired men had never spoken on it.

II. **Discussion.**
   A. What Is Baptism? Different Theories.
   1. John's Baptism.
      a. Baptized *in* Jordan. Mt. 3:5, 6.
      b. "Because there was much water." Jno. 3:23.
   2. Baptism of Christ.
      a. Baptized *in* Jordan. Mk. 1:9, 10.
      b. Came up *out of* water. Mt. 3:16.
   3. The Commission. Mt. 28:19.
      a. Convertible terms - substitute meaning of words.
   4. Under Preaching of Apostles.
      a. Baptism of Eunuch. Acts 8:35-39.
         (1) Came *unto*, went *down into*, came *up out of*.
      b. Baptism of Jailer. Acts 16:32-34.
         (1) Preached *in his house* - baptized - brought *back into* house.
      c. Baptism of Saul. Acts 22:16 - Had to *arise*.
      d. Baptism a Birth. Jno. 3:5.
      e. Baptism a burial and resurrection. Rom. 6:3, 4; Col. 2:12
      f. Baptism a planting. Rom. 6:5
      g. Baptism a washing. Heb. 10:22
   5. Blackboard Chart.

Immersion Requires	Sprinkling Requires
a. Water.	a. Water
b. Much water.	b. _____
c. Going into water.	c. _____

8

  d. Coming out of water. d. _____

  e. Birth.   e. _____

  f. Planting.   f. _____

  g. Burial.   g. _____

  h. Resurrection.   h. _____

 B. Who Should Be Baptized?

  1. Baptism of John.

   a. Confessed sins. Mk. 1:4, 5.

   b. Repentance demanded. Mt. 3:7-9.

  2. The Commission "taught" Mt. 28:19; "believe." Mk. 16:16.

  3. Under Preaching of Apostles.

   a. Pentecostians - Repent Acts 2:38; Receive word Acts 2:41.

   b. Samaritans - Believed, baptized - men and women. Acts 8:12.

   c. Eunuch - "If thou believest" Acts 8:36-38.

 C. What Is Baptism For?

  1. John's Baptism.

   a. For remission. Mk. 1:4.

   b. Unbaptized rejected counsel. Lk. 7:29-30.

   c. Flee from wrath. Mt. 3:7-9.

   d. Made exception for Christ. Mt. 3:13-17.

  2. The Commission. Mt. 28:19; Mk. 16:16.

  3. Under Preaching of Apostles. Acts 2:38; 22:16; Rom. 6:3, 4; Gal. 3:27; 1 Pet. 3:21.

III. Conclusion.

 A. Baptism a commandment. Acts 10:48.

 B. Promise to those who obey. Heb. 5:8-9; Rev. 22:14.

How To Identify The True Church

I. Introduction.

    A. Importance of the matter.

        1. Many religious bodies. Cf. Eph. 4:4 - Should know which.

        2. Some thank God for division. Jesus' prayer. Jno. 17:21; Also, 1 Cor. 1:10.

    B. Denominations are not branches.

        1. Ill. Tree bearing all kinds of fruits.

        2. Individuals are branches. Jno. 15:5.

    C. True church not denomination or sect.

        1. Word translated "sect" 5 times, "heresy" 4 times.

        2. Word "sect" never used in good sense in Bible. Cf. Gal. 5:20; Acts 24:5.

        3. Christian sect as improper as Christian heresy.

    D. Not hunt for one as "near like" it, but church itself.

II. Discussion.

    A. How Identify Anything - Characteristics.

    B. Name.

        1. Hunting for John Smith - John Jones wrong name.

        2. The Bible names. Rom. 16:16; 1 Cor. 1:2; Heb. 12:23 - not "church of Rome."

        3. Find more than one "John Smith" other characteristics - same with the church.

    C. Birthplace.

        1. Jesus to be born in Bethlehem - from any other place, an imposter.

        2. If John Smith of Springfield - John Smith of St. Louis, wrong man.

        3. Jerusalem birthplace of church. Zech. 1:16; Isa. 2:2-3; Luke 24:46-47.

        4. One founded in Eden, Mesopotamia, Sinai, wilderness of Judea - wrong one.

        5. Must not be "made in Germany," etc., but "made in Jerusalem."

D. Age.
1. If looking for John Smith of 40 years - one of 20 or 60 wrong one.
2. Man's age reckoned from birth - church from establishment. Mt. 16:18; Mk. 9:1.
3. One founded in days of Abraham, John the Baptist etc. wrong one.

E. Proper Founder - Christ. Mt. 16:18.
1. Any founded by Martin Luther, John Calvin, John Wesley, John Smith, Joe Smith - counterfeits.

F. Proper Foundation. 1 Cor. 3:11; Mt. 16:18.
1. How many churches will receive people on this proposition?
2. Many say it is not sufficient.
3. If founded on experience of men, form of government, method or ordinance - wrong foundation.

G. Proper Law.
1. Organic law of U.S. is Constitution.
2. Law governing church is Bible. 2 Tim. 3:16-17.
3. Koran, Book of Morman, Articles of Religion, Confession of Faith, Disciplines, church manuals or creeds of men are wrong laws.

H. Proper Method of Becoming Members.
1. Plan of Salvation. F.R.C.B. - added to church. Acts 2:47.
2. Cannot "join" church - God's family - born into it Jno. 3:5.

I. Proper Organization.
1. Elders and Deacons. Acts 14:23; 20:17, 28; 1 Tim. 3:1-13. No presiding elders, Arch Bishops, Popes etc.
2. Work done through church. Eph. 3:21. No missionary societies, Ladies Aids, Old Maid Conventions, etc.

J. Proper Form of Worship.
1. Prayer. Acts 2:42.
2. Singing. Eph. 5:19. No instrument.
3. Contribution. 1 Cor. 16:1-2. No pie suppers, etc.
4. Lord's Supper. Acts 20:7

III. **Conclusion**
A. Ill. Train going through tunnel bearing name "Frisco." Man on top Mt. sees trains emerge with other names.
·B. Church went into wilderness bearing all marks referred to - must come out same way.

The Lord's Supper
1 Cor. 11

I. **Introduction.**
  A. Memorial monuments erected by men.
   1. In honor of Washington.
   2. To soldiers at Nance, France.
   3. Names placed in "hall of fame."
   4. Unknown hero honored in Arlington Cemetery.
  B. God has, also, throughout the ages, left with man the memorial monument as tokens of important events.

II. **Discussion.**
  A. Some of God's Memorials.
   1. The Rainbow. Gen. 9:11-17.
   2. Pot of Manna. Ex. 16:32-34.
   3. Stones from Jordan. Josh. 4:1-9.
   4. The Passover.
      a. Memorial of deliverance. Ex. 16:32-34.
      b. Only for children of Israel throughout their generations. Ex. 12:14, 42; Num. 9:2; Ex. 12:48-49.
      c. Kept at Jerusalem. Deut. 16:5-7; 2 Chron. 30:1; Jno. 4:20-24.
      d. Jesus observed it. - under the law. Gal. 4:4.
      e. Passover called a feast. Ex. 12:14; Lev. 23:4-5.
      f. They were to cease. Hos. 2:11; Col. 2:14-16.
      g. Shadow of things to come. Col. 2:17.
      h. Christ our passover. 1 Cor. 5:7.
  B. Institution of Lord's Supper. Mt. 26:26-29; 1 Cor. 11:23-25.
   1. Used bread and fruit of vine - nothing else that passover contained. 1 Cor. 10:16.
   2. With these a new institution was made.
  C. Who Should Partake?
   1. Citizens of the kingdom. Luke 22:29-30.
   2. Must examine ourselves. 1 Cor. 11:28.

D. When Partake?
1. First day of week. Acts 20:7 - as often as first day comes.
2. Ill. "Remember Sabbath" - meant every Sabbath.
3. Contribution also on first day. 1 Cor. 16:1-2.

E. It's Importance.
1. Continued steadfastly. Acts 2:42.
2. Tarry one for another. 1 Cor. 11:33-34.
3. Forsake not. Heb. 10:25.
4. Except we eat - have no life. Jno. 6:53.
5. Worse punishment than death. Heb. 10:28-29.

F. It's Purpose.
1. Not to satisfy hunger. 1 Cor. 11:20-23. The fact that it was not full meal, distinguishes it from the passover.
2. In memory of Christ. Luke 22:19.
3. Show his death. 1 Cor. 11:26.

G. How Should We Partake?
1. Not unworthily. 1 Cor. 11:27.
2. Discern Lord's body. 1 Cor. 11:29.
3. Communion with Christ - not man - should be the heart's thought. 1 Cor. 10:16.

III. Conclusion.
A. Must observe till Christ comes. 1 Cor. 11:26.
B. Let us be sure to meet our obligation in this respect.

Bridling The Tongue
Jas. 1:26

I. Introduction.
  A. Comment on text.
    1. Religious teachers especially should bridle tongue.
    2. Must "speak as oracles of God." 1 Pet. 4:11.
  B. Should bridle mouth in presence of wicked. Psa. 39:1; Prov. 23:9.
  C. The wise and foolish distinguished. Prov. 29:11.

II. Discussion.
  A. Tongue.
    1. Make it personal - hit you and me.
    2. Ill. Master sent slave to buy best piece of meat - returned with tongue. Then for worst - tongue.
    3. Some whet their tongues (Psa. 64:3) - premeditate slander.
    4. Cannon with 80 mile range astonishes - tongue may carry deadly discharge across continent. Psa. 64:4. Need only P.O. address.
  B. Cannot be Tamed. Jas. 3:8.
    1. Ill. Three classes of beasts.
    2. Nothing but grace of God, paralysis, excision or death can silence.
  C. A Fire. Jas. 3:6.
    1. May consume all good will in a community.
    2. How great matter a little fire kindleth. Jas. 3:5.
    3. Where no wood, fire goeth out. Prov. 26:20-21.
  D. World of Iniquity - Defileth Whole Body. Jas. 3:6.
  E. Full of Deadly Poison. Jas. 3:8.
    1. As dangerous as a poison serpent. Eccl. 10:11.
  F. Blessing and Cursing From Same Mouth. Jas. 3:10.
    1. Man a freak of nature - illustrations Jas. 3:11-12.
    2. Death and life in power of tongue. Prov. 18:21.
  G. Mouth Disease.
    1. Suppose all were quarantined who have it.

2. Where do we learn it? From parents - Child speaks what he hears.
H. Example of Aaron and Miriam. Num. 12:1-13. Not so fatal today.
I. Keeping Our Tongues.
   1. We keep our soul from trouble. Prov. 21:23.
   2. May repeat something heard and be called on then to prove it.
   3. Ounce of "keep your mouth shut" worth bushel of apology.
   4. This the secret of stopping quarrels.
J. In What Ways Should Tongue Be Bridled?
   1. Tattlers - Talebearers - Gossipper.
      a. Tattlers speak thing they ought not. 1 Tim. 5:13
      b. Not go up and down as talebearer. Lev. 19:16.
         (1) Talebearer revealeth secrets. Prov. 11:13; 20:19
         (2) Whisperer separateth chief friends. Prov. 16:28; 2 Cor. 12:20.
         (3) Busybody a disorderly person. 2 Thess. 3:11; 1 Pet. 4:15.
         (4) Ask three questions before repeating a story a- Is it true? b- will it do any good to tell it? c- Will it help the person?
   2. Slander - Evil Speaking - Lying.
      a. A slanderer is a fool. Prov. 10:18.
      b. Speak evil of no man. Tit. 3:2; Jas. 4:11; 1 Pet. 2:1.
      c. Lying. Eph. 4:25; Col. 3:9; Rev. 21:8. Parents lie to children.
   3. Idle Words - Corrupt Conversation. Mt. 12:36-37; Eph. 4:29.
   4. Profanity - Cursing - Blasphemy.
      a. Scriptural references Jas. 3:9; Col. 3:8; 2 Tim. 3:2.
      b. More excuse for thief, drunkard, murderer than Blasphemer.

III. Conclusion.
A. Proper use of Tongue. Eph. 5:19; 1 Thess. 5:17.

The Temptation of Jesus
Mt. 4:1-11

I. **Introduction.**
   A. Wonderful story - nothing like it in world history.
   B. Two Adams compared.
      1. The first, a temptation, a defeat; the second, a temptation, a victory.
   C. Contrasts between His baptism and temptation.
      1. At baptism many about Him; at temptation, alone with Satan.
      2. At baptism, God spoke in approbation; at temptation, wild beasts roared. Mk. 1:10-13.
   D. The two lions meet in mortal combat. Cf. 1 Pet. 5:8; Rev. 5:5.

II. **Discussion.**
   A. Why Should Christ Be Tempted?
      1. To gird Himself for life's conflicts.
         a. About to proclaim himself humanity's deliverer Luke 4:18-19.
         b. Temptation would fit him for the work.
      2. Must prove himself Satan's superior.
         a. This inspires confidence and enlists man's cooperation. 1 Cor. 3:9.
         b. Satan can not now say Christ is untried or imperfect.
      3. To prepare way for establishment of his doctrine.
         a. Divine plan was with personal encounter with Devil.
         b. His method new: conquer His enemy by saving His foes.
      4. To Prove that man can resist temptation in strongest forms.
         a. Tempted, not as God, but as "son of man" - not divine but human nature tempted.
      5. To enable Him to succor us. Heb. 2:14; 4:15-16.

   a. As divine he knew our frailties (Jno. 2:24-25),
    but hadn't experienced them.
   b. Experience makes sympathy possible.
   c. Power of sympathy demonstrated. Mt. 21:8-9;
    27:19-25.
   d. He can plead our cause on His own experience
    of our weakness.
 B. The Extent Of His Temptations. Heb. 4:15.
  1. Three avenues of temptation. I Jno. 2:15-17.
  2. They were all used in Eden's garden. Gen. 3:6.
   Enumerate.
  3. Christ passed through them all unharmed.
 C. First Temptation. "Lust of Flesh." Vs. 3.
  1. All temptation from some lust or desire. Jas. 1:14.
   More intense the desire, greater the temptation.
  2. A 40 day fast (vs. 2) such pangs of hunger — ap-
   peals to appetite.
  3. Satan's reasons: "The son of God and starving."
  4. Christ had power to produce bread — no sin
   "within itself." Mt. 15:32-33.
  5. Christ's reply (vs. 4) cf. Deut. 8:3 — elaborate on
   language contained in it.
 D. Second Temptation — "Pride Of Life." Vs. 5-6.
  1. Devil thought a gap down — bait his hook with
   word of God.
  2. Masterpiece of Satan to take Christ to temple of
   God.
  3. "If thou be . . ." The whispered doubt again.
  4. Yielding to first temptation, lack of trust in God —
   Satan insinuates to refuse this one would be.
  5. Transforms himself as angel of light. 2 Cor.
   11:13-15. Misquotes Psa. 91:11-12. Cf. Gen. 3:4;
   and Rom. 1:25.
  6. Give Christ's reply (vs. 7). God doesn't promise pro-
   tection in rebellion.
 E. Third Temptation — "Lust of Eye." — Vs. 8-9.
  1. Kingdom of world and glory of them — describe the
   scene.
   a. Whole earth trembled under majestic tread of
    Caesars.
  2. Satan's proposition (vs. 9) didn't say "if thou be the
   son of God."
  3. Christ's reply — orders him from his presence.
  4. Imagine seeing angels gazing in astonishment —

they came to administer to Christ. Vs. 11.

III. Conclusion.
1. Lessons gleaned from incident.
   a. Skill and wisdom of Satan — attacked one on whom most depended.
   b. Satan takes advantage of necessities — attacks our weakest points.
   c. Temptation may come in pleasant suggestions.
   d. Satan doesn't always show his "cloven foot."
   e. How to resist him.
      1. Reverence for God's will.
      2. Acquaintance with God's words.
      3. The weapon — "It is written."
   f. Satan will leave if resisted. Jas. 4:7.

That Neighbor of Mine
Luke 10:25-37

I. **Introduction.**
  A. The lawyers purpose, "to try masters skill." Tempt him. vs. 25.
  B. His question.
    1. How Jesus answered, vs. 26 — turned the question.
    2. Lawyer answered with quotation from Deut. 6:5; Lev. 19:18.
    3. He knew the theory - Jesus says practice it. v. 28.
  C. Another question - "Who is my neighbor?"
    1. Neighbor question hard to keep down. Gives trouble today.
    2. Don't fill the bill - "justify ourselves," and change the subject.
    3. Jesus swapped ends with the question: "To whom am I a neighbor?"

II. **Discussion.**
  A. The Story - Relate it. V. 30-35. May have been real.
    1. Towns 20 miles apart over rocky and desolate road.
    2. Section of road called "red road" or "bloody way."
    3. Roman garrison once stationed there — dangerous yet.
  B. The Characters.
    1. The Priest. V. 31.
      a. Fortune smile upon unfortunate traveler.
      b. Man approaches who preaches love to stranger.
      c. Failed to assist - failed to be a neighbor.
    2. The Levite. V. 32.
      a. Another man of God - teacher of the law. Deut. 33:10; 2 Chr. 17:8-9.
      b. What that law requires. Deut. 22:1-4.
      c. Failed to render "first aid" - passed by on the
    3. The Samaritan. V. 33-35.
      a. Naturally expect religious men to assist, often

fail.

b. Remained for "non-churchman" to be a neighbor. Vs. 36-37. Ill. Gideon's band; Salvation Army.

c. Easy to obey that hard command - easy to love one who is good to you.

C. The Real Kernel.

1. Does "outside environment" or "inside condition," make neighbors.

2. Men were ungrateful to Him, but He was always a neighbor.

D. What Did Jesus Do?

1. When men were hungry, He fed them. Mt. 14:15-21, Mt. 15:32-39.

2. When in sorrow and trouble, He comforted them. Mt. 8:23-27; Luke 7:11-16.

3. When sick and suffering He healed them. Mt. 4:23-24; 15:30; 20:30-39.

4. When misguided He taught them. Mt. 22:29.

5. When in danger He warned them. Mt. 11:20-24; 12:41-42.

6. When going wrong He prayed for them. Luke 23:34.

F. "Go, And Do Thou Likewise." Vs. 37. Golden rule illustrated.

1. Must assist the need. Jas. 2:15-16; 1 Jno. 3:17; Gal. 6:10; Rom. 12:20.

2. Comfort the broken-hearted. Rom. 12:15; 1 Thess. 5:14.

3. Administer to the afflicted. Jas. 1:27.

4. Must teach others also. 2 Tim. 2:2.

5. Warn the unruly. 1 Thess. 5:14.

6. And pray for sinners. Mt. 5:44-47.

III. **Conclusion.**

A. Samaritan a splendid picture of Christ.

B. Let world see Jesus through you.

C. Not so much "who is my neighbor," but "am I a neighbor?"

D. Will mean much at judgment. Mt. 25:34-45.

The Great Physician
Mt. 9:10-13

I. **Introduction.**
   A. Lord manifested wisdom by revealing plan of salvation from so many viewpoints - adapted himself to various vocations.
      1. The farmer - "parable of sower" Mt. 13:3-8.
      2. The vinegrower - "parable of vineyard" Mt. 20:1-16.
      3. The fisherman - "parable of fish net" Mt. 13:47.
      4. The physician of the text.
   B. Lesson divides into four sections.
      1. The disease.
      2. The patient.
      3. The physician.
      4. The remedy.

II. **Discussion.**
   A. The Disease - Sin.
      1. It is universal. Rom. 3:23; 5:12.
         a. It originated with Adam. Rom. 5:18-19.
         b. But we gain in Christ what we lost in Adam. 1 Cor. 15:21.
      2. It will not get well of itself. 2 Tim. 2:16; 3:13. It must have a remedy.
      3. Incurable by human skill.
         a. Man has almost conquered many bodily diseases.
         b. But not soul's disease - no cure till Christ came. Heb. 10:3-4; 9:22.
      4. It is Fatal if not arrested. Jas. 1:14-15; Rom. 6:23.
         a. Some diseases may last lifetime and not kill - not so with sin.
      5. A deceptive disease - may think getting better but worse. Rev. 3:17.
      6. It is an epidemic - a contagion. Prov. 16:29, 22:24; 1 Cor. 15:33.

21

7. "Why didn't God make man so he couldn't sin?"
   a. Why not fire so it wouldn't burn; water drown, etc.

B. The Patient — Sinner.
1. *Sick man* needs physician *when* he is sick. Text.
2. Suppose he offers excuses.
   a. "Can't understand all about remedy." . . . Can't understand all the Bible.
   b. "Too sick to take remedy - get better." Not good enough to become Christian.
   c. "Afraid I'll get sick again." - Afraid can't hold out.
3. Patient must have faith in physician.
a. To add to or take from prescription shows lack of faith . . . dangerous. Rev. 22:18.

C. The Physician — Jesus.
1. To be successful must be prepared — Jesus had 4,000 years preparation. Gen. 3:16.
2. Must be acquainted with human system. Jno. 2:24f.
3. Must be acquainted with disease. Ill. by "flu."
4. Must be good judge of remedies.
5. Must be physician of ability. Mt. 11:28-30; Heb. 7:25.
6. Must be willing. Cf. 2 Pet. 3:9; Mt. 11:28; Rev. 3:20.
7. Contrasts between most physicians and Jesus.
   a. Don't visit unless sent for. Jesus did. Jno. 3:16.
   b. Don't usually come unless paid for it. Jesus did.
   c. May contract disease. Cf. Heb. 4:15.
   d. Jealous of rival. Jesus gladly took our case after others failed.
   e. Lose their patients. Jesus never did when remedy taken. 2 Pet. 1:5-10.

D. The Remedy — Gospel. Rom 1:16; 1 Cor. 15:1-4.
1. Must be taken. Bible on shelf will not cure.
2. Must be taken according to directions. Mt. 28:19-20; Mk. 16:16; Luke 24:47.

III. Conclusion.
A. If hungry man refuses to eat - starves who responsible?
B. If sick man refuses remedy - dies, who responsible?
C. Is God unjust to punish the disobedient who refuse?

Heirs of God
Rom. 8:17

I. **Introduction.**
   A. Preceding chapter closed with gloom and despair. Rom. 7:24.
   B. This one opens with note of triumph, ring of victory. Rom. 8:1-2.
   C. Variety of subjects discussed in chapter. cf. vs. 35-39.
   D. Among others he mentions "heirs of God." vs. 17.

II. **Discussion.**
   A. Children of God.
   1. Many things beyond our reach, yet we have many privileges.
   2. All cannot be rich, pretty, popular or powerful.
   3. None can be apostles or prophets . . limited number chosen.
   4. Cannot speak with tongues or work miracles, time limited. 1 Cor. 13:8-10.
   5. All cannot be good preachers, elders, singers.
   6. But all can be children of God. vs 16. 1 Jno. 3:1; Luke 10:17-20.
   7. To be children we must:
       a. Believe (Jno. 1:12)
       b. Be adopted (Rom. 8:15.)
       c. Be born again. (Jno. 3:5.)
       d. Wear family name (Acts 11:26; 1 Pet. 4:16.)
       e. Live by family government (Eph. 3:15.)
   B. Heirs of God.
   1. Suppose Henry Ford broadcast to men invitation to share his fortunes.
   2. Ill. Rush of Forty-Niners.
   3. God has invited all races of men. Rev. 22:17; Mt. 11:28-30.
       a. He owns a city eternal. Heb. 11:10; 2 Cor. 5:1; Jno. 14:1-3.

23

4. "Yet there is room" (Luke 14:22). Why? Do not believe.
C. What It Means To Be An "Heir Of God."
    1. May never know while here. 1 Jno. 3:2; Psa. 17:15.
    2. Be heir to all that God *is* or *has* . . enough for me.
    3. Some things of which we shall be heirs.
      a. Heirs of salvation. Heb. 1:14.
      b. Heirs of promise. Heb. 6:17.
      c. Heirs of grace. 1 Pet. 3:7.
      d. Heirs of righteousness. Heb. 11:7; 2 Tim. 4:8.
      e. Heirs of kingdom. Jas. 2:5; Mt. 25:34.
      f. Heirs of all things. 1 Cor. 3:21; Rev. 21:7.
      g. What more could we want? Here it is: Equal with Jesus. Rom. 8:17; "joint heirs."
D. How We Become Joint-Heirs With Christ.
    1. Must "Walk in Him." Col. 2:6.
      a. Not after the flesh. Rom. 8:1.
      b. By faith. 2 Cor. 5:7.
      c. In the light. 1 Jno. 1:7.
      d. In good works. Eph. 2:10.
      e. In His commandments. 2 Jno. 6.
      f. In love. Eph. 5:2.
      g. Worthy of Him. Col. 1:10.
      h. Finally we'll walk with Him in white. Rev. 3:4; 7:9, 13.
    2. Must "Suffer in Him." Rom. 8:17-18.
      a. Through much tribulation. Acts 14:22.
      b. Suffer for His sake. Phil. 1:29.
      c. Partakers of Christ's sufferings. 1 Pet. 4:13.
      d. If we suffer, we shall reign. 2 Tim. 2:12.
    3. Must "Live in Him." 2 Tim. 3:12; Rom. 1:17; Gal. 5:25.
    4. Must "Die in Him." Rev. 14:13.

III. Conclusion.
A. Heaven is ours by inheritance. Gal. 4:7.
B. What an inspiration to the sighing sons of a sinful race.

Heaven's King At The Door
Rev. 3:20

I. **Introduction.**
  A. The Door.
    1. Old adage: "Latchstring hangs on outside."
    2. This door has no latchstring - no latch - bar on inside.
    3. Can only be opened from within - represents heart.
    4. No power can open it without man's consent.
  B. Church at Laodicea addressed.
    1. Might apply to any heart rejecting Jesus.
    2. Why church would not open door? Condition today.
    3. Jesus once in that church. Cf. Jno. 6:45; Eph. 3:17.
    4. They drove Him out - Why? Vs. 17; Cf. Jer. 2:13 and Gal. 6:3.

II. **Discussion.**
  A. An Unusual Picture.
    1. Strange scene - describe guest who is knocking.
    2. How strange that he would visit my cabin.
    3. Would great men of earth honor us this way?
    4. Compare reception given men of earth and Jesus.
  B. Why Does Jesus Knock?
    1. Many people have their wires crossed on this.
    2. Describe how they act when asked to obey the Lord.
    3. Seem to think Jesus needs them. Cf. Jno. 15:5.
    4. Must realize our littleness and helplessness. Luke 14:7-11; Rom. 12:3.
    5. One sweet glimpse into delights of heaven, one sad peep into miseries of hell, make us realize value of soul.
    6. Jesus knows all about these things - wishes to save us.
  C. Another Crossed Wire.
    1. Many think the Lord must be coaxed - modern

revivals . . Cf. 2 Cor. 5:2.

2. God has always been willing to save. Isa. 45:22; Mt. 11:28; Rev. 22:17.
3. Question is not, will Jesus hear? but will we hear? Not is Jesus ready? but are we ready?

D. How Does Jesus Knock?
   1. Two words in text - "knock" and "voice" - Cf. Psa. 103:20.
   2. He knocks through goodness of God. Rom. 2:4.
   3. He knocks through love. Jno. 3:16; 1 Jno. 4:7-8; 3:1, 4:19.
   4. He knocks through fear. Luke 12:5; Acts 17:30-21.
      a. Speaks of death as often as life; hell as often as heaven.
      b. Talks of anguish of lost as often as bliss of the saved.
   5. Through sentiment of gospel songs. "Why not tonight?", etc.
   6. Through every gospel sermon. 1 Cor. 1:21.

E. Great Danger In Leaving Door Closed.
   1. God knocked at gates of Sodom - refused. Gen. 19.
   2. Jesus knocked at gates of Chorazin, Bethsaida and Capernaum. Mt. 11:20-24.
   3. Knocked at Pilate's door. Mt. 27:19-26.
   4. Knocked at door of Felix. Acts 24:25.
   5. Also at Agrippa's Acts 26:28.
   6. They left him on outside - at judgment He'll leave them on outside - knocking will be in vain. Mt. 25:1-12; Rev. 3:7.

III. Conclusion.
A. If Christ is on outside of your heart - you are responsible.
B. Christ, angels, friends would gladly open, but cannot. Rom. 14:12.
C. Heaven's King at your door - what will you do with Him?
D. He's at your door now - sometime you may knock at his door.
E. Will be sad when he closes his door for last time if you are on outside.

Parable of The Sower
Mt. 13:3-9

I. **Introduction.**
   A. Parable defined.
   1. Literally, placing one thing above another - a comparison.
   2. Based on facts with which people are familiar.
   B. Why Did Jesus Speak In Parables?
   1. He so often did - 38 parables recorded touching all conditions of life.
   2. The question answered by Jesus. Vs. 10-13.
      a. People must desire the truth to receive it. Cf. Vs. 14-16.
      b. Parable fits occasion - many hearing without benefit.

II. **Discussion.**
   A. One Main Point In Each Parable.
   1. Examples: Mustard seed = growth. Vs. 31-32. Virgins = watchfulness. Mt. 25:1-13.
   2. Main lesson of this. Different classes of hearers - good, better; best, bad, worse and worst.
   3. Great difference between hearts - same word had different results.
   B. The Parable Explained.
   1. The Sower.
      a. Jesus the great sower. Jno. 7:16-18; 8:26-28; 12:49-50.
      b. Sent forth apostles. Mt. 28:19-20; Mk. 16:15-16; Luke 24:46-47.
      c. Committed to faithful men. 2 Tim. 2:2.
      d. The church the pillar of truth. 1 Tim. 3:15.
      e. Compare Eccl. 11:6; Psa. 126:5-6.
   2. The Seed. Luke 8:11; Mk. 4:14.
      a. Vitality of seed
         (1) Not a "dead letter" Jno. 6:63; Heb. 4:12.

27

            (2) Incorruptible. 1 Pet. 1:23; 1 Cor. 4:15.

      b. Yields after its kind. Cf. Gen. 1:12; Gal. 6:7; Mt. 7:16; Jas. 3:12.

  3. The Soil - Human Heart.

      a. Seed falls into ground - words falls into hearts.

      b. Why some fruitful and some not? Not the seed, sower, but condition of soil. Ill. Farmer.

      c. Show the six classes of soil.

  4. Wayside Hearer. Vs. 4 - Explained Vs. 19.

      a. Do not study word - devil may suggest it is insufficient.

      b. Returning from church may stop at pool hall - fowls pick up the seed.

      c. Hard-beaten path - every rejected sermon only leaves it harder still.

  5. Stony Ground Hearer. Vs. 5; Explained Vs. 20-21.

      a. No depth of soil - not rooted and grounded, can't stand temptation.

      b. May become "offended" at those who urge him to live right - shallow impression.

  6. Thorny Ground Hearer. Vs. 7; Explained vs. 22.

      a. "Cares of world" - bad weather, crop failures, hard times, etc.

      b. "Deceitfulness of riches." Cf. 1 Tim. 6:10.

         (1) Poor man tries to get rich before serving God - obligations increase, etc.

      c. "Lust of other things." Mark 4:19.

         (1) Many of the "Other things" Cf. 1 John 2:15-17; Jas. 1:14-15.

  7. Good Ground Hearers. Vs; Explained vs. 23.

      a. No total depravity. Luke 8:15.

      b. Abound in fruits of holiness. Rom. 6:22; Gal. 5:22-23.

      c. Why harvest differed? Cultivation - Ill. farmer

III. Conclusion.

A. Give heed to things we hear. Heb. 2:2-3.

B. Take heed how ye hear. Luke 8:18.

C. This may determine our destiny.

According To The Pattern
Heb. 8:5

I. **Introduction.**
- A. Man cannot direct his steps. Jer. 10:23. Always been true.
- B. Must have chart and compass or grope in darkness.
- C. If anything is worth doing, worth doing in best way.
- D. Hence the need of reliable pattern. Ill. Seamstress and carpenter.

II. **Discussion.**
- A. Divine Pattern For Moses. Text.
  1. God uses no "cut and try" methods, but by pattern.
  2. His patterns are infinitely perfect. Man's subject to mistakes.
  3. Sanctuary and all instruments constructed by pattern. Ex. 25:9, 40. Enumerate.
  4. Moses was *faithful*. Heb. 3:5. Indicates what?
     - a. Moses a contractor, not architect - his duty to obey and construct, not to invent and plan.
     - b. Requires wisdom to plan - faith to follow plan.
- B. Solomon's Temple Built By Pattern. 1 Chron. 28:11-19.
- C. Divine Plans Unchangeable.
  1. All blessings in all ages conditioned on faithfully following God's plans.
  2. Men have attempted to change them:
     - a. Moses at rock. Num. 20:7-12.
     - b. Nadab and Abihu. Lev. 10:1-2; 16:12.
     - c. Uzzah in touching ark. 2 Sam. 6:3; Num. 4:15.
  3. Must neither add to nor subtract from. Deut. 4:2; 12:32; Josh. 1:7; Rev. 22:18-19; Gal. 1:8.
- D. Christ And The Church.
  1. Moses and Christ Compared. Heb. 3:1-6.
  2. Moses did all God commanded, so did Christ. Heb. 10:7.
  3. Christ given all authority. Mt. 28:18.

4. His greatness shown. Heb. 1:1-6.
5. Christ, gospel and church greater than Moses, law and tabernacle.
6. No change allowed in tabernacle - neither in church.
7. We are builders (1 Cor. 3:10-14). Use "measuring reed." Rev. 11:1.
8. Pattern for obtaining members.
   a. The great commission. Mt. 28:19; Mk. 16:15; Luke 24:46-47.
   b. Pattern of the confession. Acts 8:37.
   c. Pattern of baptism. Acts 8:38; Rom. 6:3-4.
9. Pattern of Organization.
   a. Elders and deacons. Acts 20:17-28; 1 Tim. 3:1ff. No Popes, Presiding Elders, etc.
   b. Church only organization. Eph. 3:21. No Missionary Endeavors, Ladies Aids, etc.
10. Pattern of Worship.
    a. Prayer. Acts 2:42. Can't substitute phonograph.
    b. Singing. Eph. 5:19. No instruments.
    c. Contribution. 1 Cor. 16:1-2. No pie suppers, ice cream suppers, etc.
    d. Lord's Supper. Acts 20:7. Neither change elements nor time.

III. Conclusion.
A. God is a *sovereign* God.
B. Christ is *head* of church. Eph. 1:22.
C. His institution is a *kingdom*, not *democracy*.
D. Hence must not trifle with His plans.

A Three-Fold Prosperity
3 John 2

I. **Introduction.**
    A. How determine man's financial standing? Not by automobile.
    B. Heart's secrets made manifest in private talks - not public speeches.
    C. May be angels at church and devils at home.
    D. Show "three-fold prosperity" suggested by the text - go hand in hand.

II. **Discussion.**
    A. The Text Explained.
        1. A lesson in values suggested.
            a. Man a two-fold being - body and soul. Mt. 10:28; Jas. 2:26.
            b. Often careful with house but neglect the inmate.
            c. Repair the building and starve the occupant — feed flesh, starve the soul. Mt. 4:4.
            d. Value of soul emphasized by Christ. Mt. 16:26.
        2. The "Wish" or prayer.
            a. Prays for health and prosperity of Gaius seems virtue in prosperity.
            b. Had he stopped here, some excuse for bending energies for wealth.
            c. Spoiled the matter for many, by "winding up" like he did. "As thy soul . . ."
            d. Soul prosperity made standard of body health and earthly prosperity.
        3. Measured by that standard.
            a. Do you pray thus for yourself and friends? — suppose prayer answered.
            b. If prospered financially as soul prospers, many in poorhouse before tomorrow.
            c. If body prospers as soul, what diseases many would have!

B. Financial Straits And Bad Health.
  1. Financial straits inconvenient and embarrassing.
     a. Are you in worse strait financially than spiritually?
  2. What is worse than bad health? - Describe.
     a. A sick soul is just as bad - or worse.
C. Spiritual Sickness And Deformities.
  1. "Religious Hydrophobia." "fear of water." cf. Mk. 16:16.
  2. Some church members have "heart trouble." Acts 8:21.
     a. "Heart contraction." 2 Cor. 6:11-13; 1 John 3:17.
        (1) "Bowels of Compassion." seat of feelings.
  3. "Spiritual fever." Lust 1 Cor. 10:6; Tit. 2:12; 1 Tim. 6:9; 1 John 2:15-17.
  4. "Rottenness of bones." Envy. Prov. 14:30.
  5. "Bloating." Pride. 1 Cor. 4:6; 5:2; 13:4; Col. 2:18.
  6. "Morbid appetite." No relish for spiritual food. Cf. Mt. 5:6; 1 Pet. 2:2.
  7. "Nearsighted." Can't see afar. 2 Pet. 1:9.
  8. "Sleeping sickness." 1 Cor. 11:30.
  9. "Deafness" dull of hearing. Mt. 13:15; Heb. 5:11-12.
  10. "Coated tongue." With slander. 1 Tim. 5:13; 4:2.
  11. "Low temperature." No spiritual zeal. Rev. 3:15; Rom. 12:11.
  12. "General debility." Good for nothing. Mt. 5:13.

III. Conclusion.
A. What should be done?
  1. Exercise in Lord's vineyard.
  2. Feast on proper food. Mt. 4:4.
  3. Take remedy of Great Physician.
B. If our soul is right we may pray for health and prosperity.

Man By Man
Josh. 7:14-18

I. Introduction.

A. Give circumstances of defeat at Ai. Josh. 6:17, 18; 7:1-6.

B. Joshua went to God in prayer. v. 6-9 - God's answer. v. 10-13.

C. Show how guilty party was found. v. 14-26.

D. Heaven's God will not tolerate sin. Ezek. 18:4.

E. Penalty on Achan severe - also Uzzah (2 Sam. 6:3-7,) Nadab & Abihu (Lev. 10:1-2,) Ananias & Sapphira. Acts 5:1-10.

F. Miniature pictures of judgment - will be taken man by man.

G. "Man by man" a practical working basis for present day problems.

II. Discussion.

A. Present Day Lessons.

    1. A job for every person.

        a. To every man *his work*. Mk. 13:34.

        b. All members necessary. 1 Cor. 12:15-22.

        c. Give parable of talents. (Mt. 25) - each man had own place to fill.

        d. Must work "according to ability" Mt. 25:15 - size of man, size of job.

        e. All cannot enter pulpit, be elders, song leaders etc., yet *work* for *all*.

    2. What can we do?

        a. Sound forth the word. 1 Thess. 1:8; Eph. 3:10.

            (1) All can and should preach. 2 Tim. 2:2; 4:2.

            (2) Individual work. Acts 8:4; 18:26; Tit. 2:3-4; Eph. 6:4.

            (3) Support those who preach. 1 Cor. 9:14.

            (4) Circulate literature that will preach.

        b. Care for sick and poor. Mt. 26:11; 1 Tim. 5:10.

        (1) Individual examples. Acts 9:36-39; Rom. 16:1-2.

        (2) When neglected, church is defamed. Cf. Salvation Army.

        (3) All can report cases to church.

      c. Hospitality and Friendliness. Heb. 13:2.

        (1) Speak to strangers in assembly.

        (2) Suppose you were a stranger. Cf. Mt. 7:12.

      d. Be present at all church services.

        (1) Interested "insiders" influence "outsiders."

B. A Church Problem.

  1. The big job - "finding work for every member."

  2. Also, "right work for right person."

  3. My (?) church may do big things - but I must be factor in the case.

  4. Not what "our church" has done - what have I done?

  5. If fail to work, judgment find us out when taken man by man.

C. Big Results.

  1. Working church can be told by its fruits. Cf. Mt. 7:16-20.

  2. Like beehive . . "not working now - better watch out." Make application.

  3. Dangerous class is the idle class. 2 Thess. 3:11; 1 Tim. 5:13.

  4. "Work" is a good remedy for carnality - will create interest.

  5. Devout, working church member never seen dancing, etc.

D. Making A Record.

  1. All sensible people wish clean record in affairs of life - business, school, etc.

  2. We are making spiritual record to be judged by. 2 Cor. 5:10.

III. Conclusion.

A. Salvation has always been an individual matter. Ezek. 14:12-20; 18:20, 30; Rom. 14:12; 1 Cor. 3:8.

B. Not saved or lost in bunches, but man by man.

C. Strength or weakness of congregation - man by man.

34

The Transfiguration
Mt. 17:1-8

I. Introduction.

A. Occurred one week after good confession. Mt. 16:18.

B. High point of apostles faith-not so high again till resurrection.

C. Mt. Tabor once thought the scene - now surrendered to Mt. Hermon.

D. Refreshing breeze from its fields of snow added calm and joy to the scene.

II. Discussion.

A. Went up In Mountain To Pray. Luke 9:28.
1. How often we read such passages. Cf. Mt. 14:23; Lk. 6:12.
2. Necessity of prayer taught by Christ and His apostles. Luke 18:1; 1 Thess. 5:17.
3. Some think Christ spent more time in prayer than teaching.
4. Why He prayed? human as well as divine - prepare for transfiguration.
5. Three with Him - were at house of Jairus (Mk. 5:37) will be in Gethsemane. Mt. 26:36.

B. The Transfiguration.
1. Disciples slept while He prayed. Lk. 9:32. Christ made the weary trip.
2. Define and describe the transfiguration. Mt. 17:2; Mk. 9:3; Luke 9:29.
3. Chariot of fire turns earthward again - two human forms in angel-like glory appear.

C. Moses The Founder of Old Dispensation.
1. Describe his life from ark of bulrushes to Pisgah's heights - from birth to death and burial.

D. Elijah Adds Awe To The Scene.
1. Not John the baptist. vs. 9-13.
2. Miraculously fed by ravens and widow. 1 Kings 17.

35

3. Slew prophets of Baal. 1 Kings 18.
4. Narrate events of 1 Kings 19.
5. His ascension to heaven. 2 Kings 2.
E. The Other Characters.
   1. Peter - bold, impetuous - gave Christian graces. 2 Pet. 1:5-7.
   2. James - gives definition of pure religion. Jas. 1:27. Discuss works.
   3. John - "son of thunder" but became "apostle of love."
F. Representatives of Time, Intermediate State, and of Heaven.
G. The Conversation. Luke 9:31 - possibly from Gethsemane to resurrection. Describe.
H. The Cloud and Voice. Mt. 17:5.
   1. Note Peter's suggestion. vs. 4.
   2. Meaning of God's statement. Cf. Heb 12:18-24; Rom. 10:4; Gal. 3:16-17, 24, 25; Eph. 2:14-16; Col. 2:14; Heb. 8:7-13.
I. Their Fear. vs. 6-7 - comfort given.
J. A Vision. vs. 9.
   1. Some say not real occurrence. Peter disputes this 2 Pet. 1:16-18.
   2. They were awake when they saw these things. Lk. 9:32.

III. Conclusion.
A. Lessons drawn from incident.
   1. Exaltation comes through humiliation. Mt. 18:4.
   2. Gospel is superior to the law.
   3. Right and wrong time to tell what should be told.
   4. A picture of the glory of heaven.

Messiah Despised and Rejected of Men
Isa. 53:3

I. **Introduction.**
   A. Messiah the perfect character.
   B. A robber preferred to Him. John 18:40. Son not reverenced. Mt. 21:33-39.
   C. Took nature of man, not angels (Heb. 2:16-17) - angels reverenced (Lk. 2:9-14) men rejected.
   D. Pretended Messiahs followed (Jno. 5:43) - true one not received. John 1:11.

II. **Discussion.**
   A. Why Despised and Rejected?
      1. The lowliness of His appearance.
         a. Became poor. 2 Cor. 8:9. This poverty contemptible.
         b. Cradled in manger (Luke 2:7) - How they expected Him.
         c. Carpenter's son (Mt. 13:55) of Nazareth. John 1:46.
         d. Men proud of worldly distinction (Mt. 23:5-6) cf. Phil. 2:7-8; Mt. 17:27; 8:20.
      2. Contempt Heightened by His claim.
         a. Styled Himself "Son of God." Jno. 5:18; 10:33.
         b. Appearance made and honors assumed seemed inconsistent. Called crazy. Jno. 10:20.
         c. Their disdain expressed. Jno. 8:53.
      3. Low State and former character of his followers.
         a. Many were poor fisherman. Jno. 21:1-2.
         b. Others had been of bad repute. Mt. 11:19; 31:32.
         c. Felt justified in their question. Jno. 7:48.
      4. Authority and Severity with which He spoke aroused rebellion.
         a. Gentle & meek - yet exposed hypocrisy of their admired characters - "fools" Mt. 23;16-17. "whited sepulchers" Mt. 23:27-28; "generation of

vipers." Mt. 23:33.
- d. Despised Him because He told them the truth. John 8:44-45.
5. Blind guides by misrepresentation led others to reject.
    - a. Took advantage of prevailing mistake. Jno. 7:41.
    - b. Claimed He broke the Sabbath. Jno. 9:13-12.
    - c. Could not deny His miracles - ascribed them to the devil. Mt. 12:24.
    - d. Would silence any who might accept Him. Jno. 9:22; 12:42.
B. Is Still Rejected Today.
  1. Jews not only ones capable of this ingratitude.
  2. Would you have so done, had you been there? Cf. Mt. 23:30.
  3. Reject Him by rejecting His words. Jno. 12:48.
C. Why despised and rejected today?
  1. Gospel rejected because of simplicity. 1 Cor. 1:18, 23; 1 Pet. 2:8.
      - a. Plan of salvation simple - "good confession" is *too simple*.
      - b. Baptism too commonplace. Cf. Luke 7:29-30.
  2. Because of its sublimity - "can't understand all" - proof of divinity.
  3. Accepted by lowly - despised by worldly great. 1 Cor. 1:26-27.
      - a. Respect wisdom of and dread to displease those "Higher up."
      - b. No wonder everywhere spoken against. Acts 28:22.
  4. Piercing rebukes of ministers. Cf. 2 Tim. 4:2-4.
  5. Because of misrepresentation. 2 Pet. 2:1-2.
      - a. When teach "wailing is not repentance" - then charged with disbelieving repentance.
      - b. "Holy Spirit through word" - charged with not believing in operation of Spirit.
      - c. "Sinner's prayer not answered" - charged with not believing in prayer.
      - d. "Baptism for remission" - charged with "water salvation," "baptizing Christians every time sin," and "infant damnation."

III. Conclusion.
A. How Rejected?

1. To refuse to believe Him as Christ (1 Jno. 4:3:3:18) or His words. Mk. 16:16.
2. Several ways: Refusing, addition, subtraction, substitution, neglecting.

B. Consequence of Rejecting Him - Heb. 10:28-29; Mt. 10:14-15.

Lessons From Four Little Creatures
Prov. 30:24-28

I. **Introduction.**
   A. We look for big things - small things beneath notice. Cf. 2 Kings 5:13.
   B. Miss some of greatest lessons - big things do not always teach biggest lessons.
   C. Wisdom of these creatures make up for their insignificance - their instinct lifts them into great respectability.
   D. To learn lessons from them may influence our whole lives.

II. **Discussion.**
   A. What the Ants Teach.
      1. Diligent preparation. v. 25; Prov. 6:6-8. Elaborate.
         a. No more industrious insect than ant - not even honeybee.
         b. None born tired - no drones, slackers or shirkers.
         c. Never go on a strike - one motto: "work."
      2. Christian worker should profit by ants wisdom.
         a. Should work during summer of life. Cf. Jer. 8:20.
         b. Lost opportunity will be regretted. Mt. 25:1-10; Luke 13:24-28; 12:16-20.
         c. Parable of vineyard (Mt. 20:1-16) - hired *laborers* - all worked - stress.
         d. Earlier we enter, more time to work - Eccl. 12:1 - more sheaves, etc.
            (1) Don't blow *ashes* in Lord's face.
         e. Winter time cometh. Gal. 6:10; Jno. 9:4 - ant sleeps in winter - not in summer.
         f. Ant doesn't store food where he may be robbed. Cf. Mt. 6:19-20; 1 Tim. 6:17.
   B. What The Conies Teach.
      1. A sure refuge. vs. 26; Psa. 104:18.

        a. Found in Mts. of Lebanon & valleys of Jordan & Dead Sea.

        b. Helpless, defenseless - would otherwise become extinct.

        c. Cleft rock is nature's safest refuge - "Cliff dwellers," also civilized people appreciate its security in storm or war.

    2. Bible abounds in figurative passages. Isa. 28:16; Acts 4:11; Eph. 2:20; 1 Pet. 2:4-5; Mt. 7:24.

    3. Our rock and refuge.

        a. Like conies we are helpless. Jer. 10:23.

        b. Our refuge must not be: lies (Isa. 28:15); ourselves (2 Cor. 1:9); wealth (1 Tim. 6:17) nor man.

        c. Our refuge is God. Psa. 94:22; 9:9; Deut. 33:27.

          (1) Coney away from refuge no more than man. Eph. 2:12.

          (2) Israel without God - was without manna, water, etc.

C. What the locusts teach.

    1. Unity and co-operation. v. 27.

        a. A plague of Egypt. Ex. 10:14-15. No plague if scattered.

        b. Profitable lesson for churches - weakness in divisions. Mt. 12:25; 1 Cor. 1:13; strength in union. Jno. 17:21-23; Eccl. 4:9-10; 1 Cor. 1:10.

        c. If they can co-operate without a king - surely we can with one.

D. What The Spider Teaches.

    1. *Fearless* labor and *perseverence*. v. 28.

        a. "taketh hold," not afraid of task - even in kings palace.

          (1) One talent man was *afraid*. Mt. 25:25.

        b. If spider fails, tries again.

          (1) Story of Bruce, Scotland's king: Lost 6 battles against English - retired to hut - despondant over Scotland's future - saw spider trying to throw thread from one beam to another - failed 6 times, succeeded 7th.

          (2) Our need of perseverence and courage. Mt. 10:28; Mt. 24:12-13.

III. Conclusion.

A. Take advantage of opportunity in summer - accept

gospel.
B. Take refuge in the "Rock of Ages."
C. Cooperate with God's people.
D. Persevere unto the end - reward is yours.

The Last Will And Testament
Heb. 9:16-17

I. **Introduction.**
   A. Define a will or testament - show what New Testament is.
   B. Last will made annuls and supercedes all others. Cf. Col. 2:11-14; Heb. 8.
   C. Necessary requirements of a legal will.
      1. Testator must be of proper age.
      2. Must be in his right mind.
      3. Must have something to give.
      4. Must be plain - making it conditional or unconditional.
      5. Must have competent witnesses.
      6. Must die before it becomes effective.
      7. After death, must be admitted to probate.

II. **Discussion.**
   A. All Requirements Possessed By Jesus.
      1. He was of proper age. Luke 3:23.
      2. He was of sound mind - never entangled by wisdom of men. Cf. Mt. 22:15-40; Jno. 7:46.
      3. He had something to give. Jno. 5:40; 10:10; 1 Tim. 1:15; 2 Cor. 8:9.
      4. He was plain with reference to conditions.
         a. Testator may make it conditional or unconditional - in either case no power can change it.
         b. Ill.: willing a farm - conditional.
            (1) Wire fence on N. side
            (2) Iron fence on E. side.
            (3) Plank fence on S. side.
            (4) Rail on W. side.
            (5) Keep fence repaired and land cultivated.
         c. Jesus made His will conditional. Mt. 7:21; Acts 10:34-35; Heb. 5:8-9; Rev. 22:14.
         d. His conditions:

43

(1) Belief. Jno. 8:21-24.

(2) Repentance. Luke 13:3

(3) Confession. Mt. 10:32

(4) Baptism. Jno. 3:5

(5) Faithfulness. Mt. 24:12f.

5. He chose competent witnesses.

   a. Two or three are sufficient. Deut. 17:6; 2 Cor. 13:1.

   b. But He chose twelve. Luke 24:45-48; Acts 1:8; 10:40-41.

6. His will ratified by his death. Heb. 9:16-17.

   a. While testator lives may dispose of property as he chooses - after death the will must be met. Ill. $1,000. to two boys.

   b. Jesus gave rich gifts while alive. Mt. 9:1-2; Lk. 23:43; but we can't be saved that way *after* He died.

7. Will probated and executed after His death.

   a. Probate court at Pentecost. Acts 2.

      (1) No blessing offered as Jesus had bestowed them during His life.

      (2) But conditions expressly mentioned - two vs. 38.

   b. Other examples of its executions.

      (1) The Eunuch. Acts 8:26ff - three conditions expressed.

      (2) Saul. Acts 9 & 22 - one condition expressed.

      (3) Cornelius. Acts 10 - one condition.

      (4) Jailer. Acts 16 - Two conditions expressed.

   c. The fifth condition - faithfulness. Heb. 3:14.

III. Conclusion.

A. The will can never be changed - it must stand.

B. No man can claim the inheritance who has not obeyed.

C. Untold riches are offered - will you accept?

The Second Coming of Christ
John 14:2-3

I. **Introduction.**

A. Many false theories, yet coming a reality.

B. A vital, comforting Bible doctrine.

C. If I could not believe it, could not believe He ever lived or died.

D. Why I believe: Jno. 14:2-3; Acts 1:11; 2 Thess. 1:10; Rev. 1:7; 2 Cor. 13:1.

II. **Discussion.**

A. Contrasts In His Two Advents.

　　1. Babe in a manger (Lk. 2:7) - King on Throne. Mt. 25.

　　2. In likeness of men (Phil. 2:7) - In glory of God. Mk. 8:38.

　　3. In flesh to save (Heb. 2:14) - In spirit to judge. 2 Tim. 4:1.

　　4. As a servant (Mt. 20:28) - As a Lord of lords. 1 Tim. 6:14, 15.

　　5. As sin-offering (Heb. 10:5, 12) - "Without sin unto salvation (Heb. 9:28).

B. When Will He Come?

　　1. His coming mentioned so often.

　　2. Apostles laid special emphasis on it.

　　3. Jesus left monument with inscription, "Till He comes." (1 Cor. 11:26).

　　4. No date was ever set. Cf. Mt. 24:36; Rev. 16:15.

C. Why Will He Come?

　　1. To be glorified in saints. 2 Thess. 1:10.

　　2. To raise dead and change living. 1 Cor. 15:51, 52.

　　3. To judge world. Acts 17:31; 2 Tim. 4:1; Jude 14-15.

　　4. To reward according to works. Mt. 16:27; 25:41-46; Rev. 22:12.

　　5. To receive His people. Jno. 14:2-3; 1 Thess. 4:17.

　　6. To take vengeance on wicked. 2 Thess. 1:8-9.

　　7. These prove He is not coming to establish a

kingdom. Cf. Mic. 4:8; 1 Cor. 15:24.

D. How Will He Come?
1. With shout, and trump of God. 1 Thess. 4:16.
2. With 10,000 saints. Jude 14; 1 Thess. 4:14.
3. With mighty angels. Mt. 25:31; 2 Thess. 1:7.
4. In power and great glory. Mt. 24:30.
5. In flaming fire. 2 Thess. 1:8.
6. In clouds of heaven. Rev. 1:7; Acts 1:9-11; Mt. 26:64.

E. Duty And Clouds Often Associated.
1. In Old Testament - clouds token of divine presence and majesty.
   a. Led Israel by cloud by day and fire by night. Ex. 13:21.
   b. In a cloud God met Moses at Sinai. Ex. 24:16.
   c. In tabernacle - "appeared in cloud upon mercy seat." Lev. 16:2.
   d. Thus the Jews thought of God as using them as a vehicle of conveyance. Psa. 104:3; Isa. 19:1.
2. New Testament - same sacred association.
   a. Bright cloud at transfiguration. Mt. 17:5.
   b. Jesus left earth in a cloud. Acts 1:9.
   c. Will return same way. Acts 1:11.
   d. When we leave earth for heaven, will leave in clouds. 1 Thess. 4:17.

III. **Conclusion.**
A. To Bible lovers, the rainbow is a pledge and promise. Gen. 9:11-16.
B. May clouds have sacred meaning to us - one will be Lord's chariot.
C. Always live in expectation of His coming. 2 Pet. 3:3-4; Luke 12:45-46.

The Judgment
Heb. 9:27

I. **Introduction.**
  A. Every subject has dark and bright side - a fire will warm or destroy; water quench thirst or works devastation.
  B. Two appointments in text - God will keep them.
  C. First sentence terrible - through Adam. Gen. 3:19; Rom. 5:12.
  D. Sin, death and judgment inseparable - follow in succession.
  E. Probation ends with death. Luke 16:19-31.

II. **Discussion.**
  A. Certainty Of Judgment.
    1. Conscience teaches a judgment to come.
    2. Proven by unjust situation - Rich man & Lazarus." Luke 16.
    3. Scriptural statements: Rom. 2:12, 16; 2 Cor. 5:10; Acts 17:31.
      a. Not a matter of *choice* - many would be destroyed like beasts if it were.
  B. When Will It Be?
    1. May be chastened now Heb. 12:6 - not "the judgment."
    2. Condition of each known now to God (Jno. 3:18; 2 Tim. 2:19) - but may change.
      a. Judgment day not a trial with witnesses - "pronouncing sentence."
    3. In the future Acts 24:25; Heb. 10:26-27.
    4. After death. Heb. 9:27; Rev. 20:11, 12.
    5. When Christ comes. Jude 14, 15; 1 Cor. 4:5.
    6. On resurrection day. Jno. 11:24; Mt. 11:23-24.
    7. When world burns. 2 Pet. 3:7-10.
  C. Who Will Be Judged?
    1. Fallen angels. 2 Pet. 2:4; Jude 6.
    2. The wicked. 2 Pet. 2:9; 3:7.

3. God's people. Heb. 10:30;
4. All men. Rom. 14:10-12; Mt. 25:32.
5. Living & dead included. 2 Tim. 4:1.
6. Nothing will exempt: wealth, fame, etc. Elaborate. Cf. Mt. 10:15; 11:22; 12:41-42.

D. Who Will Be The Judge?
1. The Son of God. Jno. 5:22; Acts 10:42; Acts 17:30;
2. Hence it will be "righteous" Rom. 2:5; "Just" John 5:30; "true" Rev. 16:7.
3. No bribing the judge. Prov. 11:4; 2 Chron. 19:7.

E. How Shall Men Be Judged?
1. Word of God the Standard. Psa. 96:13; Jno. 12:48; Jas. 2:12.
2. Our lives compared with the standard. Mt. 12:36-37; 2 Cor. 5:10; Rom. 2:5-6. Note the "books."

F. Results Of The Judgment.
1. Separation into two classes. (Mt. 25:31-33) - don't have to be as bad as some.
2. Two sentences.
   a. An invitation to glory. Mt. 25:34.
   b. A denunciation to torment. Mt. 25:41, 46.

III. Conclusion.
A. Who shall be able to stand.
B. Preparation must be made here. Amos 4:12.
C. Brevity and uncertainty of life, certainty of death and judgment demand haste.

Partakers of Divine Nature
2 Pet. 1:3-4

I. **Introduction.**
    A. Common expression: "that's human nature," "according to nature," etc.
    B. Some have a devilish nature. Eph. 2:3; Jno. 8:44.
    C. But there's a higher "divine nature" - comment on text.
        1. "Corrupt" vs. 4.
        2. Design of promises. vs. 4.
        3. Adequate provisions. vs. 3.
    D. In creation, body came from earth. Gen. 2:7; 3:19; 1 Cor. 15:47; but spirit from God. Zech. 12:1; Eccl. 2:7; Heb. 12:9.
    E. "Divine nature" in this sense universally possessed - but "divine nature" of text is conditional. Explain.

II. **Discussion.**
    A. What Christianity Does.
        1. The great work is to make men like Christ - Christ like.
        2. Corrupt being, out of place in angel's presence.
        3. Must have "divine nature" to enjoy divine society.
        4. True in this life, sinners and saints.
        5. Christianity changes the nature - fits for society of saints and joys of heaven.
          a. But still has human nature can fall. 2 Pet. 1:5-10.
          b. Does not become God or angel - still a man.
    B. Theory and Practice.
        1. Is the theory practical - will it work?
        2. A Case: "Love enemies" Mt. 5:44 - contrary to human nature.
        3. Not contrary to divine. Jno. 3:16; Rom. 5:10; Luke 23:34; Cf. Acts 7:60.
    C. Some Items of Divine Nature.
        1. Love. 1 Jno. 4:7-8 - a prominent attribute of God.
          a. May thus practice "golden rule." Mt. 7:12.

b. Love works no ill. Rom. 13:10; 1 Cor. 13:5.
   (1) If universally practiced, no locks, no prisons, firearms, armies, etc.

2. Holiness. Psa. 145:17. All moral principles in God's nature.
   a. Chastens us that we might partake. Heb. 12:10.
   b. Cannot see - "enjoy" Lord otherwise. Heb. 12:14. Imagine reprobate in God's presence.
   c. Other statements. 1 Pet. 1:15-16; Eph. 4:29; 2 Pet. 3:11.

3. Righteousness. Psa. 111:3.
   a. Partake by "putting on new man." Eph. 4:24.
   b. Must do righteousness. 1 Jno. 2:29; 3:7.
   c. Must exceed Pharisees. Mt. 5:20.
   d. All Bible promises for righteousness. Cf. Mt. 25:46.

4. Mercy. Luke 6:36; Eph. 2:4; Psa. 103:17.
   a. Jesus taught mercy by precept & example - Mt. 5:7; 18:33; Lk. 10:30-37; Mt. 14:14.
   b. Mercy not inconsistent with Justice. Jas. 2:13.

5. Longsuffering and Patience. Psa. 86:15; Num. 14:18; Rom. 2:4.
   a. Punishment deferred because of this. 1 Pet. 3:20; 2 Pet. 3:9.
   b. We must partake of this. Eph. 4:2; Gal. 5:22.

6. Forgiveness. Dan. 9:9; Psa. 96:5.
   a. Demonstrated by Jesus. Luke 24:34; Isa. 53:12.
   b. We must forgive. Eph. 4:32; Mt. 6:14-15.
   c. Human to err, but divine to forgive.

III. Conclusion.

A. Consequences of "corrupt nature" are terrible.
B. "Divine nature" brings untold blessings.

Walking Worthy of God
1 Thess. 2:11-12

I. **Introduction.**
  A. Comment on text. Cf. Col. 1:10; Eph. 4:1-2.
  B. These indicate when may walk worthy or unworthy of their profession.
  C. Scoffers ridicule pretending church members - God's blasphemed.
  D. Hypocrisy great hinderance - hiding place for sinners.
  E. World full of strange doctrines - truth needs to be stressed.
  F. Beneath it all, right living needs to be emphasized by practice.,

II. **Discussion.**
  A. How God's name Is Blamphemed.
     1. Among Gentiles through you. Rom. 2:24.
     2. David's sin. 2 Sam. 12:14, and Israel's transgressions. Ezek. 26:16-20.
     3. Not practice what we preach. Mt. 23:1-4; Rom. 2:1-3; 14:22.
  B. How To Walk Worthy Of God.
     1. In Conversation. Phil. 1:27.
        a. Examples in such. 1 Tim. 4:12; 1 Pet. 1:15; 2 Pet. 3:11.
        b. No profane language. Eph. 4:29; 5:4.
        c. Honest conversation. 1 Pet. 2:12.
        d. Sound speech - not condemned. Tit. 2:8.
     2. In good works. Eph. 2:10; 1 Pet. 2:12; 1 Tim. 2:10; Col. 1:10.
        a. After God's commandments. 2 Jno. 6.
           (1) Lord's day worship. Heb. 10:25.
           (2) Study. 2 Tim. 2:15. Not approved otherwise. Col. 1:10.
           (3) Kindness. Heb. 13:2.
        b. With Patience. Jas. 5:7; Heb. 10:36.

        c. In Love. Eph. 5:2.
           (1) How? 1 Jno. 5:2-3; 1 Jno. 4:20; Luke 6:46.
    3. In His steps. 1 Pet. 2:21.
        a. How He walked. Jno. 8:29; Cf. 1 Jno. 2:6; 3:22.
    4. Must walk with God.
        a. Enoch walked with God 300 years - Gen. 5:22 - God honored him. v. 24.
        b. Living illustration. Mt. 24:13.
        c. Noah walked with God. Gen. 6:9.
        d. If men of worldly renown invite us to walk with them, how would we act?
C. Why Many Walk Unworthily.
    1. Some do not realize their real condition. Cf. Rev. 3:17.
    2. Some try to serve two masters. Mt. 6:24.
    3. Others rely on own strength.
        a. Cf. David. 1 Sam. 17:37, 45.
    4. Others are neglectful. Cf. Heb. 2:3.
        a. Intend to help orphans - but neglect.
        b. Intend to help preachers - but neglect.
        c. Intend to meet regularly - but neglect.

III. Conclusion.
A. What is worth while? Money? Education? Power? Good Time?
B. Note Solomon's conclusion. Eccl. 12:13.
C. Faithfulness - not numbers - counts in service of God.
    1. Gideon's army reduced from 32,000 to 300 - kind God wanted. Judg. 7:1-7.
    2. 30 faithful members better than 300 not converted.

Our Creed
2 Tim. 3:16

I. Introduction.
A. Church of Christ often charged with having creed.
B. "Creed" from "credo" - "I believe" - must have creed if believe anything.
C. What I am is result of what I believe. Prov. 23:7.
   1. If believe in Democratic party - and so vote - am Democrat, etc.
   2. Same with doctrines of Mrs. Eddy, Chas. Russell, Joe Smith.
   3. But "faith alone" will not make anything out of me. Jas. 2:22-24.

II. Discussion.
A. Facts Worth Considering.
   1. No church, society, organization, party can exist without foundation.
   2. "Foundation" is "creed" - Republican & Democrat parties.
   3. Church of Christ could not exist without a creed.
B. Human Creeds Wrong.
   1. All creeds are not wrong - but *man made* religious creeds are.
   2. Objections to human creeds.
      a. They are not inspired of God.
      b. They do not meet the needs of the whole world.
      c. They are not perfect.
      d. They must be revised every few years.
      e. They teach many things contrary to word of God.
      f. They will not be standards of judgment.
   3. Church of Christ has no human creed - distinction here.
      a. Divine creed divides people. Mt. 10:34-36; Lk. 12:51-53; 2 Cor. 2:16.
      b. It also unites. Acts 4:32.

53

C. One Lawful Creed.
    1. As creeds are foundations compare 1 Cor. 3:10-11.
    2. Apostles had but one subject or foundation: Christ. Acts 2:36; 8:5, 12.
    3. Men required to believe in Christ. Acts 16:31. "Their Creed."

D. The Bible As Our Creed.
    1. It is inspired of God. 2 Tim. 3:16-17.
    2. It meets the needs of the whole world. Mk. 16:15.
    3. It is perfect. Psa. 19:7; Rom. 12:2; Jas. 1:25.
    4. It needs no revision. 1 Pet. 1:25.
    5. It will be the standard of judgment. Jno. 12:48.

E. Some Principles Taught Therein.
    1. All things created - not evolved. Gen. 1:20-27.
    2. The church a New Testament institution. Mt. 16:18; Col. 2:14.
    3. People born into world innocent. Mt. 18:1-3; 19:14.
    4. The Gospel is God's saving power. Rom. 1:16.
    5. God hears only the righteous. 1 Pet. 3:12; Jno. 9:31.
    6. Salvation is conditional. Heb. 5:8-9; 2 Thess. 1:7-8.
    7. Baptism is essential. Mk. 16:16; 1 Pet. 3:21.
    8. Baptism is a burial. Rom. 6:3-4.
    9. Man may fall from grace. 1 Cor. 10:12; Gal. 5:4.
    10. "Christian" a divinely given name. 1 Pet. 4:16.
    11. Salvation in church. 2 Tim. 2:10.
    12. Two places of eternal destiny. Mt. 25:46.

III. Conclusion.
A. This creed will admit of no tampering. Rev. 22:18-19.
B. Note the things for which it is profitable. 2 Tim. 3:16f.
C. Our slogan: "Where the Bible speaks, we speak; and where the Bible is silent, we are silent."

Where Art Thou?
Gen. 3:9

I. **Introduction.**
  A. Relate story of Adam's transgression. Gen. 3:1-7.
  B. "Hid themselves" vs. 8 - How like man!
  C. A pointed question. vs. 9 - twofold meaning: bodily and spiritual whereabouts.
  D. Man a twofold being. 2 Cor. 4:16 - body and soul - dwell in variety of houses.
  E. Address of body is one thing, address of soul is another.

II. **Discussion.**
  A. Living in Pleasure.
    1. A merry widow described. 1 Tim. 5:6. Fits others.
       a. Gives herself to pleasure at theatres, card parties, ballrooms.
       b. Revelry and frivolity she calls "life" - but she is dead.
       c. Regardless of cost in money, health, reputation, goes giddy gait.
       d. Finger of God erases "life" and writes "death". Cf. Rev. 3:1.
    2. The Rich describes. Jas. 5:5; Cf. Luke 16.
       a. Pleasures of sin "for a season." Heb. 11:25 Ill. The Judas tree.
    3. Pleasures that must be avoided.
       a. Those about which you may doubt. Rom. 14:23.
       b. Those that would lead others to sin. Rom. 14:15; 1 Cor. 8:9.
       c. Those that have the appearance of evil. 1 Thess. 5:22.
  B. Living In Malice And Envy. Tit. 3:3.
    1. Things become as we think (Rom. 14:14) — others may look like rascals.
    2. "Hateful and hating one another." Cf. Prov. 15:17.

3. Leads to retaliation: Cain (Gen. 4:4-8); Joseph's brothers (Acts 7:9); Saul (1 Sam. 18:8); Herodias (Mk. 6:19-29); Princess of Babylon (Dan. 6).

C. Abiding In Darkness. Jno. 12:46; 1 Jno. 2:11.
   1. Body may live at "Sun-Light Inn", but soul in darkness.
   2. Why some live at this residence. Jno. 3:19-20.

D. What It Means to Dwell in Love.
   1. Must love God. 1 Jno. 4:19; 1 Jno. 5:3.
      a. Transgression of greatest law, the greatest sin. 1 Jno. 3:4; Mt. 22:36-40.
   2. Must love enemies. Mt. 5:44; Rom. 12:17-21.
   3. Must love one another. 1 Jno. 3:11; 4:11.
      a. Will prefer each other. Rom. 12:10; Gal. 6:10.
      b. Will manifest kindness. Eph. 4:32. Imagine Christians refusing to speak. Cf. 1 Jno. 4:20; Acts 22:7-8; Mt. 25:34-45.
      c. Will forgive trespasses and misunderstandings. Mt. 6:12-15.
      d. Will tell each other of faults. Mt. 18:15. Not tell others.
      e. Try not to offend. Jas. 3:2; Prov. 18:19.

III. Conclusion.

A. Where art thou today? In God's family or out?

B. If in His family, are you near to Father or "afar off"?

C. Are you in path of duty or on mountain of sin?

D. Where you live here will determine where you will live hereafter. Jno. 5:28-29.

Conversion
Acts 3:19

I. Introduction.
   A. Define "Conversion." "To Turn." Acts 26:20; Cf. Mt. 5:39.
   B. Necessity of conversion.
      1. Emphasized by text. Elaborate.
      2. Other references. Mt. 18:1-3; Jas. 5:19-20.

II. Discussion.
   A. Is Man Active or Passive?
      1. Some say, "Wholly an act of God." Who responsible for the lost?
      2. Another extreme: "Man does it all." Jer. 10:23.
      3. The truth is both are active. 1 Cor. 3:9.
         a. Both parts shown: Jno. 3:16; Eph. 2:8-9; Mt. 13:15 - Emphasize.
   B. A Threefold Change.
      1. Heart must be changed. Acts 15:9.
         a. Intellect, sensibility & will with all their functions.
         b. Life must be changed. Mt. 3:8.
         c. State or relationship must be changed. Col. 1:13; Rom. 6:4.
         a. Ill.: "Law of naturalization" - every step must be completed.
      4. "Conversion" sometimes embraces whole process. Mt. 18:3; Sometimes part of it. Acts 11:21; 26:20.
   C. Essential Steps of Conversion.
      1. Cannot turn *to* one thing without turning *from* another - illustrate.
      2. If never turned in wrong direction no occasion to turn other.
      3. Essential steps in turning from or to God are the same.
         a. Adam & Eve turned wrong direction by definite

steps. Gen. 3.
  (1) Preacher *preached* a lie - Eve *heard* it.
  (2) She *believed* a lie.
  (3) She *obeyed* a lie.
  (4) She became *guilty* - was not condemned by *faith only.*
  (5) God drove her out and closed gates.
  b. In man's return same steps must be taken.
  (1) Gospel must be *preached* and *heard.* 1 Cor. 1:21-23; Psa. 19:7. Jno. 6:45 - hence God uses agents and instruments. Jno. 16:7; 20:22-23; Acts 26:18; Jas. 5:20.
  (2) Must *believe* truth - Jno. 20:30-31.
  (3) Must *obey* truth - 1 Pet. 1:22.
  (4) God pardons us.
  (5) Receives us back into His family.
D. Difference Between Conversion and Pardon.
  1. Conversion takes place in mind of man - Pardon in mind of God.
  2. Man cannot tell by feelings whether pardon has been granted.
  3. Ill.: man in prison feels he is pardoned, regrets crime, but gates do not open; pardon takes place with Governor - he must sign the pardon before the prisoner is freed.
E. Our Fault If Never Converted.
  1. Peoples heart waxed gross. Mt. 13:15; Acts 28:27.
  2. "Ye *would not.*" Mt. 23:37.
  3. "Ye *will not* come." Jno. 5:40.

III. Conclusion.
A. God provided the plan - we must be converted His way. Isa. 55:7-9.
B. Other ways may seem right, but lead to death. Prov. 14:12.

Conversion of the Eunuch
Acts 8:26-39

I. **Introduction.**
   A. Preachers today relate modern day conversations.
   B. Two classes from which to choose - modern cases and Bible cases.
   C. Bible cases under divine supervision twice - when done and when written.
   D. Rule and example simplify matters - Ill: 'Partial payments.'
   E. Whole book of examples given us - *Acts*.

II. **Discussion.**
   A. The Man To Be Converted.
      1. Treasurer of Queen Candace - great authority v. 27 position of trust.
      2. Either Jew or proselyte - "for the worship." v. 27.
      3. Traveled 1,000 miles in chariot - lesson for us today who put business before religion.
   B. The Preacher - Philip The Evangelist.
      1. Angel spoke to preacher - not to sinner. v. 26.
         a. Note command given & how God directed their travel.
      2. When he arrived Holy Spirit spoke to him - not to sinner. v. 29.
   C. Eunuch Was Reading.
      1. Was reading aloud - Philip heard him. v. 30.
      2. Usually find people reading today when traveling.
      3. But what do they read? - The Bible?
      4. Philip's manner of introducing himself. v. 30. No formalities - *butted right in.*
      5. We might take offence at like question - possibly Philip could tell he was troubled.
      6. The eunuch's request. v. 31.
      7. His question. Vs. 32-34. No unbelieving Jew can answer. None could without revelation of Christ.

59

D. Philip Preached Jesus - How?
  1. If I preach some man - tell of his ancestors - incidents of life - last sayings and death.
  2. To preach Jesus, tell of ancestry; birth; baptism; temptation; miracles; betrayal; trial; death; burial; resurrection; last charge; commission; ascension. Elaborate.
  3. "Why not preach Christ, leave out baptism?" have to leave off both ends of the story. Mt. 3 and 28:19.
E. What He Did.
  1. "What hinders?" how he knew - Today we ask: "Is there any way out of it?"
  2. His confession. V. 37 - break in story to leave it out.
      a. A confession is required. Rom. 10:9-10; 1 Jno. 4:15.
      b. "All the heart" embraces intellect, sensibility and will.
  3. His baptism - how performed? V. 38-39.
      a. "Desert" - not without water (Two Gazas - one depopulated). Cf. Mt. 14:13.
  4. Rejoiced after baptism v. 39 - no man ever rejoiced over sins forgiven before baptism under great commission.
F. Suppose We Meet Him.
  1. Ask why wet and rejoicing - relates experience.
  2. Would he tell about angel and spirit?
  3. Relate story as he would tell it.
G. Suppose Makes Excuses.
  1. Don't know just what my relatives would say.
  2. Might lose my job.
  3. Be back at Jerusalem next year - may accept then.
  4. Come to Ethiopia, convert my family - then I am ready.

III. Conclusion.
A. Does your conversion correspond with this? Did you hear, believe, confess, go into water, etc.?
B. If not, you should change it.

Conversion of Saul
Acts 9:1-19

I. **Introduction.**
   A. Bible a book of biographies.
   B. Paul most prominent man of N.T. except Jesus.
   C. Most heroes soon forgotten - Paul unobscured by the lapse of centuries.

II. **Discussion.**
   A. History And Character Of Saul.
      1. Born of a great race - Acts 22:3; Phil. 3:5.
      2. Educated under Gamaliel. Acts 22:3.
      3. Religious from youth. Acts 26:4-5.
      4. Inspired with zeal. Gal. 1:14; Acts 22:3.
      5. Persecuted the church. Gal. 1:13; 1 Tim. 1:13.
         a. Imprisoned disciples. Acts 8:3; 22:4.
         b. Compelled them to blaspheme. Acts 26:11.
         c. Voted to kill them. Acts 26:10; 7:58; 22:20.
         d. Went even to strange cities. Acts 26:11; 9:1-2.
      6. Was conscientious, but wrong. Acts 23:1; 24:16; 26:9.
      7. The chief of sinners. 1 Tim. 1:15.
   B. His Vision.
      1. Saw a light from heaven. Acts 26:13.
      2. Heard voice of Christ. Acts 26:14.
      3. These were to qualify him for an apostle. Acts 22:14-15; 26:16-18; 1 Cor. 9:1.
      4. We need not expect these in our case - it never so occurred in any other case.
   C. His Conversion.
      1. Was convinced by Christ's words - believed.
      2. Christ failed to speak peace to him. Acts 9 - Why?
      3. Emphasize *must*. Acts 9:6.
      4. Allowed him to remain in agony three days. Acts 9:9 - Repentance.
      5. Preacher sent to him. Acts 9:10-17.

6. Commanded to be baptized. Acts 22:16.
   a. Didn't say, "I'm a church member." "One is as good as another," etc.
   b. His agony passed away. Acts 9:18-19.
D. Why Did He Embrace Christianity.
   1. Not for wealth. 1 Cor. 4:11-12; Acts 20:33-34.
   2. Not for reputation. 1 Cor. 4:13.
   3. Not for power. 1 Cor. 15:9; 2 Cor. 4:5.
   4. Not to commit fraud.
      a. His companions would have exposed him.
      b. No man would suffer as he, for a fraud. 1 Cor. 15:19.
   5. Not because deceived - no human could produce the vision.
   6. Not from "over-enthusiasm" - vision would have been opposite.
   7. But because he knew whom he believed. 2 Tim. 1:12; 1 Pet. 4:19.

III. Conclusion.
A. A Surrendered Life.
   1. Persecutor becomes persecuted. 2 Cor. 11:23-27.
   2. Singleness of purpose. Phil. 3:13.
   3. Always faithful. Acts 20:26-27.
   4. Left no unfinished business. 2 Tim. 4:6-7.
      a. Relatives may finish earthly affairs for us - not spiritual.
   5. Describe his death.

Conversion of the Samaritans
Acts 8:1-25

I. **Introduction.**
   A. History of the city and race. 1 Kings 16:23-24; 2 Kings 18:9; 17:22-29.
   B. Points leading to the lesson.
      1. A great persecution. Acts 8:1.
      2. Apostles remain in Jerusalem. Acts 8:1.
      3. Others scattered and preaching. Acts 8:1, 4.

II. **Discussion.**
   A. The Preacher - Philip.
      1. Not apostle but the evangelist. Acts 8:5; 6:1-6; 21:8.
      2. His work as deacon terminated by dispersion of the church.
   B. What He Preached. V. 5.
      1. Christ the burden of preaching if inspired men. 1 Cor. 2:2; Gal. 6:14.
      2. "Christ," "gospel" and "word" the same. 1 Cor. 2:2; 15:1; Acts 8:25.
         a. Compare "preaching Moses" Acts 15:21.
   C. Preach Christ - Let Other Folks Alone.
      1. Must preach Him fully (Acts 20:20, 27) This will antagonize others.
         a. As "Son of God" Mt. 16:18 - Antagonize infidels.
         b. As "Savior" Tit. 2:13-14 - antagonize Universalists.
         c. As "saving the obedient" Heb. 5:9. Antagonize Calvinists.
         d. As "God's Prophet" (teacher to man) Acts 3:22. What he taught - antagonize sectarians.
         e. As "High Priest" Heb. 3:1 - antagonize ecclesiastical priesthoods.
         f. As "king" 1 Tim. 6:15 - explain kingdom, territory, subjects, conditions - antagonize many.
   D. Results Of Philip's Preaching.

1. People under spell of magician - unfavorable for gospel reception. v. 9-11.
   a. Magic & miracles compared - one to excite the curiosity, other benefit to humanity.
   b. Vast difference seen by people. v. 6.
   c. Miracles to confirm the word. Mk. 16:20; Heb. 2:2-4.
2. Great joy in the city. v. 8 - Why?
3. What the people did.
   a. Believed & baptized v. 12. Cf. Mk. 16:15-16.
   b. How learn of baptism?
   c. No infants - "believed - men and women" v. 12.
   d. No "church" consulted about their baptism.
   e. Simon also converted. v. 13-14; Cf. Mk. 16:16.

E. Visit Of Peter And John. V. 14.
   1. Purpose of visit - impartation of Spirit. v. 15.
   2. Had fallen on none. v. 15 - not a prerequisite to baptism or salvation.
   3. Why the miraculous endowment?
      a. Apostles needed inspiration - revealing God's will.
      b. In absence of apostles, others needed miraculous aid - revelation incomplete.
   4. How imparted? v. 17 - never conferred by others. Hence ceased.

F. Simon's Sin. V. 18-19.
   1. Not "yet" in bond of iniquity. v. 21, 23. Apostasy.
   2. Only one sin mentioned - "this thy wickedness" vs. 22.
   3. Not "alien sinner's" prayer v. 22-23 - two laws of pardon.

III. Conclusion.

A. Meetings today must be like Samaria.
   1. If not, it is not right.
   2. If like it, it is right.
B. Circumstances may differ.
   1. Philip had miraculous gifts - no New Testament.
   2. I have New Testament - not the gifts.

Conversion of Lydia
Acts 16:6-15

I. **Introduction.**
   A. Pay tribute to woman in care for man from birth to death.
   B. Woman's position before Christ - "slave" - same today in heathenism.
   C. Many women mentioned in Bible - remarkable for vices or virtues.

II. **Discussion.**
   A. History of Lydia.
      1. Home in Thyatira, Asia - 300 miles away - famed for purple dyes.
      2. Seller of purple: v. 14 (used only on costly goods) Lk. 16:19. intimates wealth.
      3. God wants "business people" - Moses-Ex. 3:1-4; Gideon-Judg. 6:11-12; David-1 Sam. 16:11-12; Matthew-Mt. 9:9; Peter-Mt. 4:18-19; Luke-Col. 4:14.
      4. Jew or proselyte - "worshipped God" v. 14 - even among heathen.
         a. Business affairs didn't make her worldly.
         b. Kept sabbath.
            (1) Competition didn't cause her to open shop. Lesson for us on Lord's day.
            (2) Had she been less faithful, none to report. Some faithful at home only.
         c. Kept the custom of praying. v. 13 - though no man to lead.
      5. Yet needed conversion - Why?
   B. How Preachers and Sinners Were Brought Together.
      1. Forbidden to preach in Asia or Bithynia. v. 6-7.
      2. Paul's vision at Troas. v. 8-9. Europe calling to Asia.
         a. Greatest help to any nation is gospel.
      3. "Endeavored to go" v. 10 - ships seldom sailed from Troas to Macedonia.

65

4. "Straight course" v. 11 - wind and sail vessels.
   a. Two days for journey. v. 11 - 5 days on return. Acts 20:6.
   b. Not luck - God working.
5. Why not "direct operation"? - earthen vessels. 2 Cor. 4:7.
6. Went to prayer meeting - could have gone to show; dance. etc.

C. The Sermon.
   1. Such simplicity - not even a pulpit. v. 13.
   2. The old, old story from Abraham to Christ.

D. The Effect Of The Sermon.
   1. She heard. v. 14 - Importance of hearing. Jas. 1:19.
   2. Lord opened her heart. v. 14.
      a. What is the heart? Thinks, Mt. 9:4; Reasons, Mk. 2:8; Understands, Mt. 13:15; Believes, Rom. 10:1; Condemns, 1 Jno. 3:20.
      b. Why it needed opening:
         (1) Not to enable her to hear (heard first) - explain "attended" v. 14.
         (2) Not totally depraved - closed by Jew's conception of Christ. Cf. 1 Cor. 1:23.
      c. How was it opened?
         (1) Not by direct operation. Cf. Rom. 10:17; Acts 14:27; 15:7-9.
   3. She believed. v. 15; Cf. Heb. 11:6.
   4. Was baptized. v. 15. Cf. Mk. 16:16.

E. Were Infants Baptized?
   1. "Household" doesn't necessarily include infants. I Sam. 1:21-22.
   2. To prove infant baptism, must prove:
      a. That Lydia was married.
      b. That she had children.
      c. That she had them with her.
      d. That they were too young to believe.
      e. That they were baptized.

III. Conclusion.
A. The gospel addressed to hearts of men.
B. If you would be saved, let it be opened.

Conversion of the Jailor
Acts 16:16-34

I. **Introduction.**
  A. Paul & Silas on second missionary tour - vision at Troas. v. 9.
  B. Prayer meeting - conversion of Lydia. v. 13-15.
  C. Doing nothing to excite people or disturb peace of city.

II. **Discussion.**
  A. The Unfortunate Damsel.
    1. Held in double bondage - masters and demons. v. 16.
    2. Making merchandise of her misfortune - Cf. White slave trade.
    3. She testified truthfully. v. 17. Cf. Mk. 5:7.
    4. Why did Paul reject her co-operation?
       a. Would have placed demons and apostles in alliance.
       b. Good repute of apostles reflected on demons & vice versa.
    5. Evil spirit cast out. v. 18.
    6. Paul might have asked her masters: Have you no interest in womanhood? Virtue? Humanity?
  B. Preachers Falsely Accused. v. 19-21.
    1. Many a man has suffered unjustly.
    2. To have stated fact would reflect credit on Paul.
    3. Justice disregarded - no opportunity to defend themselves.
    4. Stripped - commanded to be beaten. v. 22 - by men they came to bless.
  C. The Imprisonment.
    1. Solemn charge to jailor at peril of his life. v. 23.
    2. Not treated as common criminals. v. 24 - Describe stocks.
    3. They carry their case to a higher court. v. 25.
       a. Men do not pray when enraged or sing in

67

distress.

       b. Strange sounds in heathen prison - all hear.

D. The Earthquake - God's Vindication. v. 26.
1. Describe it - slamming of doors, clanking fetters, etc.
2. Jailor attempts suicide. v. 27-28. Why?
3. Fell trembling before preachers. v. 29. Good attitude for prayer.

E. His Question. v. 30.
1. Not saved from terrors of earthquake - passed.
2. Not saved from Roman penalty - prisoners there.
3. But saved from divine condemnation.
4. What must *I do*? - Not God, Christ, H.S. - not what must *I feel*?

F. The Answer. v. 31.
1. Took him where they found him - a pagan, cf. Pentecostians & Saul.
2. Not faith only - knew nothing of Christ - how believe Cf. Jno. 9:36; Rom. 10:17.
3. Word of Lord preached. v. 32 - what included? Isa. 2:2; Luke 24:46-47; Acts 2:38.
4. Clearly implied that he repented. v. 33.

G. His Baptism. v. 33.
1. Its importance - same hour.
2. How performed: Not in jail. v. 30; not in house v. 33-34.
3. Rejoiced afterwards. v. 34.

H. Were Infants Baptized?
1. Word spoken to all. v. 32.
2. All believed. v. 34.

III. Conclusion.
A. The Macedonian call more fully realized.
B. Paul's experience agreed with his instruction. Phil. 4:6-7.

Conversion of Cornelius
Acts 10

I. **Introduction.**
   A. Gospel universal in application. Mt. 28:19; Mk. 16:15.
   B. For all conditions and classes of humanity - bad and good.
   C. This story interesting because a Gentile.
   D. Very few Jews ever hear gospel now.

II. **Discussion.**
   A. Characteristics of Cornelius.
      1. Was a "Centurion" - military officer. v. 1.
      2. He was "devout." v. 2. Not usually true of military officers.
      3. Had a reverent family. v. 2.
      4. Charitable - "gave alms." v. 2.
      5. Prayed always. v. 2.
      6. Just and of good report. v. 22.
   B. The Angel's Visit - *Miracle No. 1* - v. 3-6.
      1. Prayers were heard. Cf. v. 31.
         a. For what had he been praying? Bible doesn't say.
            (1) If "heard" = "answered" - not for salvation, for he believed 4 days later. Acts 15:7.
            (2) His prayer "for memorial" - in remembrance of promise. Gen. 12:1-3.
      2. To be told what he ought to do. v. 6.
         a. May seem there is nothing he ought to do.
         b. Regardless of his goodness he was unsaved. Acts 11:14.
         c. No man ever saved on account of his intrinsic worth. Tit. 3:5.
      3. Why didn't angel tell him? - save 60 mile trip & 3 days waiting?
      4. Note the angel's plainness.
      5. Why angel appeared: N.T. not written - told him.

C. Peter's Vision - *Miracle No. 2*. v. 9-16.
  1. Men on way to Joppa. v. 7-9.
  2. Had preached only to Jews. Gentiles as dogs. The vision convinced him. v. 11-16.
  3. Spirit assists in same matter. v. 19-20 - *Miracle No. 3*.
  4. Peter goes with six brethren. v. 23; 11:12.
D. Meeting At Home Of Cornelius
  1. Peter refuses to be worshipped. v. 25-26.
  2. Refers to dangerous step taken. v. 28-29.
  3. Cornelius related experience. v. 30-32 - What modern churches would do.
  4. Many present "to hear all things commanded." vs. 33.
      a. To want to learn the truth, important thing.
  5. Peter's sermon. v. 34-43.
E. Falling Of Holy Spirit - *Miracle No. 4*. v. 44; 11:15.
  1. Why did it fall?
      a. Not to save him - Acts 11:13-14.
      b. Not to give faith - Acts 15:7.
      c. Not to purify heart. Acts 15:9.
      d. Not to give remission of sins. Acts 10:43.
      e. Not to purify soul. 1 Pet. 1:22.
      f. Not to convert. Psa. 19:7.
      g. Not to sanctify. Jno. 17:17.
      h. But to convince Jewish brethren. Acts 10:44-47; 1 Cor. 14:22; and others at Jerusalem. Acts 11:15-18.
      i. If saved when H.S. fell, saved before faith. Cf. Acts 15:7; 11:15.
F. How Converted?
  1. Eliminate miracles - like all others.
      a. Not now needed as all those things have been settled.
  2. What he did.
      a. Heard the word. Acts 10:33.
      b. Believed. Acts 15:7;
      c. Repented Acts 11:18;
      d. Baptized Acts 10:48; Cf. Acts 11:1; 2:41.
      e. No infants included. Cf. Acts 10:33, 44, 46.

III. Conclusion.
A. Take Cornelius as example of honesty.
B. Must be converted like he was.

Conversion of the Three Thousand
Acts 2

I. **Introduction.**
   A. Interested in new things.
   B. Gospel had been preached in promise (Gen. 3:8), prophecy (Isa. 53), preparation (Mt. 3:3).
   C. But this the beginning in *fact* - death, burial, resurrection.

II. **Discussion.**
   A. The Day - Pentecost.
      1. Pentecost - Jewish feast - 50 days from sabbath of passover. Lev. 23:15-16.
      2. Days great because of events. July 4th.
      3. Events of this: church established, gospel began, Holy Spirit received.
   B. The City - Jerusalem.
      1. Larger cities in history - Babylon, N.Y., London, none greater.
      2. Sacred associations: Solomon reigned, Jesus suffered, etc.
      3. God had appointment for 700 years for this time & place. Isa. 2:2-3; Mic. 4:1-2; Luke 24:46-49, Acts 1:2-5.
   C. The Crowd.
      1. Time since ascension spent in prayer. Acts 1:14.
      2. Great crowd from Parthia to Rome. Acts 2:9-11 - not for preaching but feast.
   D. The Coming of Spirit. v. 2-4.
      1. Not to the multitude. v. 6.
      2. Not to the 120. Acts 1:26; 2:37. Cf. Acts 1:2-5.
      3. Effect on multitude. v. 6-8 - Different today.
      4. "Pouring" not mode of it, but method of bringing element & candidates together.
   E. The Preacher - Simon Peter.
      1. Often wonder if preacher is big enough for occa-

71

sion.
  2. Had received keys of kingdom. Mt. 16:19; 28:19.
  3. Though once a traitor - proves to be right man - guided by the Spirit.
F. Peter's Sermon.
  1. Replied to charge of drunkenness. v. 14-21. Explain.
  2. Jesus approved by miracles - ye know. v. 22. No proof needed.
  3. Him you have crucified. v. 23. No proof needed.
  4. Delivered by predetermined counsel of God. v. 23.
     a. The proof:
        (1) David predicted the resurrection of some one. v. 25-28.
        (2) Shows this refers to Christ. v. 29-31.
        (3) That he could not refer to himself . . v. 34-35. Cf. Mt. 23:43-44.
  5. He was raised. v. 24.
     a. The proof.
        (1) They were witnesses. v. 32.
        (2) Was exalted - didn't see Him - but promise fulfilled. v. 33.
  6. His conclusion.
G. Results Of The Sermon.
  1. Pricked to hearts. v. 37. How? "They *heard*."
  2. Their question. v. 37 - Its import.
  3. The commands given. v. 38. Elaborate on "for remission."
     a. People pray for Pentecostal shower - note what these preached.
  4. Gift of Spirit. v. 38. Not miraculous. Cf. Acts 8:18.
  5. The extent of the promise. v. 39.
  6. Obedience rendered. v. 41.
     a. Easy to immerse 3,000 in one day.
     b. Plenty of pools could be used for purpose - pool of Siloam is 50 ft. long & 16 ft. wide.

III. **Conclusion.**
  A. Do you believe Peter preached a full gospel?
  B. If 3,000 could understand it in one discourse, can you?
  C. The promise is to the obedient. Heb. 5:8-9.

The Precious Word
1 Sam. 3:1

I. **Introduction.**
   A. Comment on the text.
   B. Things appreciated when scarce - material things.
      1. When scarce, price goes up - cotton, etc. Adage: "you never miss water."
      2. Value determined by amount obtainable: - Banks closing doors, famines, etc.
   C. "Famine of hearing word." Amos 8:11-12. Cf. Dark ages.
   D. Why called "precious word"? Points in lesson will explain.

II. **Discussion.**
   A. David's Language. Psa. 139:17.
      1. How know His thought? Cf. Job 11:7; 1 Cor. 1:21; Rom. 11:34.
      2. Faith produced is a "precious faith." 2 Pet. 1:1.
   B. The Only Standard.
      1. Creeds of men are fallible - gospel is perfect. 2 Tim. 3:16-17.
      2. The only means of determining: right or wrong, saint or sinner, obedience or disobedience, true worship or vain worship.
   C. God's Saving Power.
      1. The power of God to save. Heb. 4:12; Rom. 1:16; Jas. 1:21.
      2. Begotten by it. 1 Cor. 4:15; Jas. 1:18.
      3. Made clean through it. Jno. 15:3.
      4. Sanctified by it. Jno. 17:17.
      5. Will make us free. Jno. 8:32.
      6. Will be judged by it. Jno. 12:48.
   D. Reveals Plan of Salvation.
      1. The first principles. Acts 16:31; 17:30; Rom. 10:9-10; Acts 2:38.

2. Christian living. 2 Pet. 1:5-7.
3. Think of consequences with plan unrevealed.
E. Reveals Coming Judgment & Doom of Sinners.
    1. Scriptural statements. 2 Cor. 5:10, 11; Heb. 9:27; Rev. 21:8.
    2. Otherwise no preparation would be made - "How precious."
F. It Gives Assurance.
    1. Scriptural statements. 1 Thess. 1:5; Acts 17:31; Col. 2:2.
    2. A feeling of security when we have solid ground.
G. Foundation of Hope. Rom. 15:4; Col. 1:23.
    1. Without it would be "most miserable" 1 Cor. 15:19.
    2. We sigh for sinless, summerland - to meet loved ones.
    3. Every aim, desire, hope based on what is written.
H. Its Precious Promises. 2 Pet. 1:4.
    1. Promises effect us according our faith in the one who promises, and their value.
        a. He that promised is faithful. 2 Pet. 3:9; Heb. 10:23.
        b. Their value cannot be estimated.
            (1) Remission of sins. Heb. 8:12.
            (2) All things work for good. Rom. 8:28.
            (3) Glorious resurrection. Rom. 8:11; 1 Cor. 15:44.
            (4) Mansion in God's house. Jno. 14:1-3.

III. Conclusion.
A. Must either accept or reject the Bible.
B. Let us lean upon it - not deceive or mislead.
C. If sad, read it,

> For "here a blessed balm appears
>   To heal the deepest woe,
> And those who read this Book in tears,
>   Their tears will cease to flow."

Prayer
1 Thess. 5:17

I. **Introduction.**
   A. Necessity of prayer.
   1. We are children of God. 1 Jno. 3:1 - gracious privilege to pray.
   2. Also solemn duty - no Christian life without it. 1 Thess. 5:17.
   3. Jesus who "did no sin" (1 Pet. 2:22) prayed often - our example.
   B. What is prayer?
   1. Not a cold, formal observance - but talking to God. Communion.
   2. Expression of heart's desire. Rom. 10:1; Phil. 4:6.
   3. A "coming of the throne of grace." Heb. 4:16.

II. **Discussion.**
   A. Does God Answer Prayer?
   1. If not, no one made better or happier through prayer.
   2. Scriptural statements. Mt. 7:9-11; 21:22; Jno. 14:14; 1 Jno. 5:15.
   B. Why Are Not All Prayers Answered?
   1. He answers prayers like He saves - on conditions.
   2. The Conditions.
      a. Must be righteous. 1 Pet. 3:12 (Cf. 1 Jno. 3:7; Psa. 119:172;) 1 Jno. 3:22; Jno. 9:31; Prov. 15:8, 29; 28:9; Psa. 66:18; 1 Tim. 2:8; Jno. 15:9.
      b. Must pray in faith. Jas. 1:6-7. Cf. Mt. 21:22.
      c. Must pray according to His will. 1 Jno. 5:14; Cf. Luke 22:42.
         (1) This means "in harmony with His word." Cf. Num. 12:13-16.
      d. Must pray in name of Christ. Col. 3:17; Jno. 14:13-14; 15:16.
      e. Must endeavor to keep peace. Mt. 5:23-24.

       f. Must forgive. Mark 11:25-26.

       g. Must be unselfish and sincere. Jas. 4:3; Mt. 6:5; Jas. 5:16-18 - help answer our prayer.

C. Secret Prayer.
1. Public prayer enjoined. 1 Tim. 2:8.
2. Secret prayer important. Mt. 6:5-6.
3. All can thus pray - no chance for hypocrisy.

D. For Whom Should We Pray?
1. We need to pray for ourselves.
2. Must not be selfish - pray for brethren. Jas. 5:16; 2 Thess. 3:1.
3. Should pray for enemies. Mt. 5:44-46 - Explain how pray for sinners. Rom. 10:1.
4. Should pray for rulers. 1 Tim. 2:2.
5. In fact, for all men. 1 Tim. 2:1.

E. Humility In Prayer.
1. Should be like the publican. Luke 18:11-13; Psa. 9:12.
2. Examples of humility in prayer: *Solomon* - 1 Kings 8:54; *Ezra* - Ezra 9:5-6; *David* - Psa. 95:6; *Daniel* - Dan. 6:10; *Jesus* - Luke 22:41; *Paul* - Acts 20:36.
3. Ill. Man breaking stones on knees.
4. Should show reverence. Heb. 12:28 - eliminate talking and laughing.

III. Conclusion.

A. Praying should not cease. Text.
B. Will always need to pray in this sinful world.
C. It can only cease to swell praise on Canaan's happy shore.

Doing God's Will
Mt. 7:21

I. **Introduction.**
   A. Bible religion is a doing religion.
      1. Christ came with this in view. Jno. 6:38; Heb. 10:5-7.
      2. Man must meet the demand "Do." - Eccl. 12:13; Jas. 1:22-25; 1 Pet. 4:19; Heb. 12:20-21.

II. **Discussion.**
   A. Importance of Doing God's Will.
      1. Can't enter kingdom otherwise. Text.
      2. Makes us members of God's family. Mk. 3:35.
      3. Causes God to hear our prayers. Jno. 9:31.
      4. Fits us to receive the promises. Heb. 10:36.
      5. Causes us to abide forever. 1 Jno. 2:17.
      6. Prepares us for heaven. Rev. 22:14.
      7. It seems with such importance attached, all would do His will - but many things keep them from it.
   B. Theories That Keep People From Doing.
      1. Theory of Universalism.
         a. Contrary to Bible. Mt. 7:13-14; Heb. 5:8-9.
         b. But if convinced that *all* will be saved, no need to do His will.
      2. Theory of Predestination.
         a. Contrary to Bible. 2 Pet. 3:9; Acts 10:34-35.
         b. But if convinced their destiny settled, no need to do His will.
      3. Total Depravity Theory.
         a. Contrary to Bible. Mt. 18:3; Jno. 5:40.
         b. But if convinced they are so dead can't act, no need to try.
      4. Theory of Direct Work of Spirit in conversion.
         a. Contrary to Bible. Psa. 19:7; Rom. 1:16;
         b. But if convinced they can't act till God sends it; had as well wait.

77

5. No Hell Theory.
   a. Contrary to Bible. Mt. 25:41, 46; 13:41-42.
   b. But if convinced no future punishment, they go on in sin.
6. Second Chance Theory.
   a. Contrary to Bible. Mt. 25:1-13.
   b. But if convinced second chance will be given - wait for it.
7. Can't Fall Theory.
   a. Contrary to Bible. 1 Cor. 10:12; Gal. 5:4; 2 Pet. 2:20-21.
   b. But if convinced can't fall - they neglect.

C. Commandments Embraced In God's Will.
   1. To the sinner.
      a. Belief. Jno. 6:40; Heb. 11:6;
      b. Repentance. 2 Pet. 3:9; Acts 17:30.
      c. Confession. Mt. 10:32.
      d. Baptism. Mk. 16:16; Acts 10:48.
   2. To the Christian. 2 Pet. 1:5-7 - Enumerate.

III. Conclusion.
A. His will is perfect. Rom. 12:2.
B. It should be done from the heart. Eph. 6:6; Rom. 6:17.
C. Our actions prove whether we are wise or foolish. Mt. 7:24-27.

Watch
Mark 13:37

I. **Introduction.**
   A. Have word "watch" written in Chinese style —
   B. Christ many times enjoined "watchfulness."
      Luke 12:35-39.
   C. Likewise did the apostles. 1 Cor. 16:13; 1 Thess. 5:6.
      4. So much would not have been said without some reason for it.

II. **Discussion.**
   A. Why Should We Watch?
      1. Because the devil has power to tempt. Mt. 4:1-11; 26:41; 1 Thess. 3:5; Gal. 6:1.
      2. Because Satan is active. 1 Pet. 5:8; 2 Tim. 2:26.
      3. Because Satan is as a minister of light. 2 Cor. 11:13-15; Col. 2:8.
      4. Because of our ignorance of second coming of Christ. Mk. 13:32-37; Mt. 25:1-13; Rev. 16:15.
      5. That we might be able to stand. Luke 21:36.
   B. What Should We Watch?
      1. Words
         a. Should not offend in word. Jas. 3:1-12.
         b. Words should be fitly spoken. Prov. 25:11.
         c. Must account for idle words. Mt. 12:36-37.
         d. Should not engage in filthy conversation. Eph. 4:29; 5:4.
         e. Vain babblings will eat like a canker. 2 Tim. 2:16-18.
      2. Actions.
         a. Lord weighs actions. 1 Sam. 2:3.
         b. Will be judged by our actions. 2 Cor. 5:10; Rev. 20:11-12.
         c. Actions determine our destiny. Heb. 10:28-29.
            (1) Hypocritical acts injure cause of Christ.
            (2) Acts of love are evidence of discipleship.

Jno. 13:35.
3. Thoughts.
   a. Wicked should forsake his thoughts. Isa. 55:7-9.
   b. Should be brought to obedience. 2 Cor. 10:4-5.
   c. What we should think upon. Phil. 4:8.
4. Company.
   a. We become like our associates. 1 Cor. 15:33.
   b. Solomon warned son against bad company. Prov. 1:10-15.
   c. May get a snare to our souls. Prov. 22:24-25.
   d. Beware of evil workers. Phil. 3:2; 2 Pet. 3:17.
5. Heart.
   a. All issues of life from heart. Prov. 4:23.
      (1) Our words. Mt. 12:34.
      (2) Our actions. Prov. 16:9.
      (3) Our Thoughts. Mt. 15:19; Prov. 23:7.
      (4) Our company. Prov. 16:9.
   b. If fountain is pure, stream will be; if heart is pure, issues of life will be.

III. Conclusion.
A. Finally we should watch in all things. 2 Tim. 4:5.
B. If we fail to watch, results are sad. Rev. 3:3.

Foolish Things
1 Cor. 1:27

I. **Introduction.**
  A. This lesson doesn't concern foolish things people do.
  B. But things God has done that people think are foolish.
  C. May think preaching is "foolishness" - God's plan. 1 Cor. 1:21.
  D. Even "Christ crucified" was foolishness to some. 1 Cor. 1:23.
  E. But "foolishness of God is wiser than men." 1 Cor. 1:25.

II. **Discussion.**
  A. Some Things The World Considers "Foolish."
   1. Building of the Ark - relate the story. Gen. 6:5-17.
      a. Noah preached to the people. 2 Pet. 2:5.
      b. It had never rained (Gen. 2:6) So a flood seemed foolish.
      c. Give construction of ark - certain material and size seem foolish.
   2. Moses smiting Rock - relate story. Ex. 17:1-6.
      a. To strike water from a rock seems foolish.
      b. No power in rod, but in obedience.
   3. Scape Goat - relate story. Lev. 16:7-10, 20-22.
      a. Placing sins on goat's head seems foolish - but God's plan.
      b. No power in goat - but in doing God's will.
      c. People today would call it "goat salvation."
   4. Brazen Serpent - relate story. Num. 21:1-9.
      a. To look at brass snake to heal snake bite seems foolish.
      b. No power in snake to heal bite - but in obedience.
      c. People today would call it "snake salvation."
   5. Walls of Jericho - Relate story. Josh. 6:1-16.
      a. Man's wisdom would say "dynamite walls."
      b. God said "march around" - seems foolish.

        c. Power came by doing what God said.
    6. Naaman's Leprosy - Relate story. 2 Kings 5:1-14.
        a. Dipping in Jordan to heal leprosy seems foolish.
        b. Naaman thought something else would do as well. v. 12.
        c. No power in the water, but in obedience.
    7. Blind Man - relate story. John 9:1-7.
        a. Restoring sight that way seems foolish.
        b. No power in spittle, clay or water, but in obedience.
B. Some Foolish Things That Concern Us.
    1. Baptism. Mk. 16:16; Acts 2:38.
        a. Some ask: What power in water to forgive sins?
            (1) As much as in "scape goat" under law of Moses.
            (2) As much as in "brazan serpent" to heal snake bite.
            (3) As much as in "water of Jordan" to heal leprosy.
            (4) No power in either, but in obedience.
        b. Baptism despised and considered base by some. Cf. 1 Cor. 1:28.
    2. Lord's Supper.
        a. Looks foolish because don't eat enough to satisfy hunger.
        b. But God has chosen it - we must obey.

III. **Conclusion.**
    A. Don't decide against a thing because it seems foolish.
    B. It may *seem foolish* to do what God says, we *know it is not* to do so.

Nearsighted Christians
2 Peter 1:9

I. **Introduction.**
   A. Define "nearsighted."
   B. Comment on text - If "can't see afar off" must be near-sighted.
   C. Men have always thought of present and neglected the future.

II. **Discussion.**
   A. Old Testament Examples of Nearsightedness.
      1. Essau Selling Birthright.
         a. Relate the story. Gen. 25:27-34.
         b. By being nearsighted he lost:
            (1) Double portion of goods. Deut. 21:17.
            (2) Blessing given Jacob. Gen. 27:1-40.
            (3) Right to be ancestor of Christ. Gen. 26:4.
            (4) Mention of his name many times where Jacob's is.
      2. Trespass of Achan.
         a. Relate the story. Josh. 6:17-18; 7:1-26.
         b. By being nearsighted Israel lost battle, v. 1-5.
         c. And he lost his life. v. 25.
      3. Disobedience of Saul.
         a. Relate the story. 1 Sam. 15:1-21.
         b. By being nearsighted, God rejected him as king 1 Sam. 15:22-28.
   B. New Testament Examples.
      1. Ananias and Sapphira.
         a. People were giving their possessions. Acts 4:34-37.
         b. They kept back part - lost life. Acts 5:1-10.
      2. Simon The Sorcerer.
         a. Obeyed gospel. Acts 8:5-13.
         b. Nearsighted in trying to purchase gift. Acts 8:14-19.

        c. Had to repent. Acts 8:20-23.
    3. Church of Corinth in Corrupting Lord's Supper. 1 Cor. 11:20-34.
    4. Church of Laodicea in becoming lukewarm. Rev. 3:14-17.
  C. How We May Be Nearsighted.
    1. By failing to study Bible. 2 Tim. 2:15; Heb. 5:12-13.
        a. Ill. Bro. Wolfe "smelling of book."
        b. Not simply a preacher duty.
    2. By neglecting the assembly. Heb. 10:25, 28, 29; John 6:53.
    3. By failing to contribute. 1 Cor. 16:1-2; 2 Cor. 9:8f.
    4. By seeing others faults instead of own. Mt. 7:1-5.
    5. By returning evil for evil. Rom. 12:17-21; Mt. 6:14-15.
    6. By not loving brethren. 1 John 2:11; 4:20.
    7. By thinking too much of self. Rom. 12:3.
    8. By having interest centered on worldly things. 1 John 2:15-17.
    9. By backsliding. 1 Tim. 1:15; 1 Tim. 4:1; 2 Pet. 2:20-21.

III. Conclusion.
  A. The Remedy. 2 Pet. 1:5-7.
    1. Define each of the seven Christian graces.
    2. When these are applied, nearsightedness disappears.

Escape For Thy Life
Gen. 19:17

I. **Introduction.**
   A. This espression signifies there is danger. Cf. Mt. 23:33; Rom. 2:3.
   B. It also suggests that escape is possible. Cf. 1 Cor. 10:13; Psa. 124:7.

II. **Discussion.**
   A. Old Testament Examples.
      1. Lot and Wife - Relate the story., Gen. 19.
         a. Life offered in the mountain. v. 17.
      2. Noah and Family - Relate the story. Gen. 6.
         a. Life offered in ark. v. 18.
      3. Israel Leaving Egypt - Relate story. Ex. 14.
         a. Salvation offered by crossing sea. v. 13-15, 30.
      4. Disobedient prophet - Relate story. 1 Kings 13.
         a. Life offered by going a certain way. v. 9-10.
   B. To Where Must We Escape For Life?
      1. Lot and wife could flee to mountain - We can flee to Mount Zion. Heb. 12:22; Isa. 46:13.
      2. Noah escaped in ark - we in ark of Christ or church.
         a. Some similarities between ark and church.
            (1)*One builder:* Noah builder of ark. Gen. 6:13; Christ builder of church. Mt. 16:18.
            (2)*One building:* Just one ark. Gen. 6:14; Just one church. Eph. 4:4; Col. 1:18.
            (3)*One kind of material:* Ark of Gopher wood; Church of baptized believers. Gal. 3:26-27.
            (4)*One way to enter:* One door in ark. Gen. 6:16; Christ door of church. Jno. 10:7-8.
            (5)*One source of light:* One window in ark. Gen. 6:16; Word of God light of church. Psa. 119:104.
      3. Israel crossed Sea - We crossed sea of baptism. 1 Cor. 10:1-2; Mark 16:16.

      4.   Prophet had a certain way - We to Christ our way. Jno. 14:6; Jno. 1:4; 2 Tim. 2:10.
C. How May We Escape Into Christ?
      1.   Believe *unto*. Rom. 10:10.
      2.   Repent *unto*. Acts 11:18.
      3.   Confess *unto*. Rom. 10:10.
      4.   Baptized *into*. Gal. 3:27.
D. From What Must We Escape?
      1.   From temptation. 1 Cor. 10:13.
      2.   From pollution of world. 2 Pet. 1:4; 2:20.
      3.   From idolatry. 1 Cor. 10:14.
      4.   From indifference. Rom. 12:11.
      5.   From profanity. 2 Tim. 2:16-17.
      6.   From vulgarity. Eph. 4:29; 5:4.
E. Why All Do Not Escape.
      1.   Some refuse to obey. Heb. 12:25.
      2.   Some neglect their salvation. Heb. 2:3; 1 Thess. 5:2-3.
      3.   Some are hypocrites. Mt. 23:33.
      4.   Some are deceived. 2 Pet. 2:18-19.
      5.   Some are liars. Prov. 19:5.

III. **Conclusion.**
A. By properly acting here we will escape at judgment bar. Luke 21:36.
B. To fail to escape there will be a sad thing. 2 Thess. 1:7-9.

A Christian
Acts 26:28

I. **Introduction.**
    A. A name given to disciples of Christ. Acts 11:26.
    B. One of which we should feel no shame. 1 Peter 4:16.
    C. Must mean something or Agrippa would not have been almost persuaded - Text.

II. **Discussion.**
    A. What Is It To BE A Christian?
        1. In "faith" - A "believer in Christ." Jno. 20:30-31; Acts 16:31.
        2. In "relationship" a "child of God." Jno. 1:11-13; Gal. 3:26.
        3. In "communion" - a "friend of God." Jno. 15:14-15; Cf. Jas. 4:4.
        4. In "character" - a "saint." 1 Cor. 1:2; 2 Thess. 1:10.
        5. In "conflict" - a "soldier." 2 Tim. 2:3-4.
        6. In "this world" a "pilgrim & stranger." 1 Pet. 2:11.
        7. In "obligation" - a "follower of Christ" Mt. 10:38; 1 Pet. 2:21; 1 Cor. 11:1.
            a. How follow? Him? By doing as He did.
                (1) Revile not & threaten not. 1 Pet. 2:23; Rom. 12:17-21.
                (2) Forgive. Lk. 23:34; Mt. 6:14-15.
                (3) Be about God's business. Lk. 2:49; Mt. 25:14-31.
                (4) Do God's will. Heb. 10:7; Lk. 22:42; Mt. 7:21 - Prayerful; - Student of Bible; - Attend the worship; - Care for poor; - Give as prospered.
    B. What Does It Cost To Be A Christian?
        1. Always count the cost of an undertaking. Lk. 14:28-32.
        2. It cost Jesus His Life. Mt. 20:28; Heb. 2:9-10.
        3. It cost God His Son. John 3:16.

4. It cost us:
    a. Forsaking of all. Lk. 14:33; Mt. 10:37.
    b. Self denial. Mt. 16:24.
    c. A life of sacrifice. Rom. 12:1-2.
    d. A life of work. Gal. 5:6; Phil. 2:12.
    e. A life of suffering. 2 Tim. 3:12; Mt. 5:11; 1 Pet. 4:16.
C. Does It Pay To Be A Christian?
    1. Chief consideration of an enterprise is "does it pay."
    2. Doesn't pay to remain lost. Mt. 16:26.
    3. Devil, sinners, hypocrites and backsliders may say it doesn't pay.
    4. All Christians agree that it does. Cf. Mt. 5:12; Rom. 8:16-18; 2 Cor. 4:17; 1 Pet. 1:4; Rev. 21:4.

III. Conclusion.
A. Life is brief and uncertain. Cf. Jas. 4:14.
B. "Almost persuaded" will not save.
C. Heaven will rejoice over one who fully decides to be a Christian. Lk. 15:7-10.

The New Name
Isa. 62:2

I. **Introduction.**
    A. Is there anything in a name?
       1.   Call man "liar" who says not, and watch results.
       2.   Ill. Woman shouting, "Glory to Beelzebub."
       3.   Bible evidence. Acts 4:12; Prov. 18:10.

II. **Discussion.**
    A. God Has Always Named His People.
       1.   Adam - Gen. 5:1-2.
       2.   Abraham - Gen. 17:5.
       3.   Israel - Gen. 32:28; 2 Kings 17:34; Deut. 28:10; (Heb. El = God).
       4.   Not unreasonable to expect the same now.
    B. Prophecy Referring To The Name - Enumerate each point.
       1.   An everlasting name. Isa. 56:5.
       2.   Another name. Isa. 65:14-15.
       3.   Name for the heathen. Amos 9:8, 11, 12; Acts 15:14-17.
       4.   A new name. Isa. 62:2-3.
    C. The Prophecy Fulfilled.
       1.   Jew to cry for sorrow of heart (Isa. 65:14); Fulfilled. "Jews wailing place."
       2.   Name to be a curse (Isa. 65:15); Fulfilled; "Jew, hiss and byword."
       3.   Jewish kingdom to be slain (Isa. 65:15; Amos 9:8); Fulfilled: At cross (Eph. 2:14-16.)
       4.   Tabernacle of David to be rebuilt (Amos 9:11); Fulfilled: Christ on David's Throne (Acts 2:29-31).
       5.   Gentiles to see God's righteousness (Isa. 62:2); Fulfilled: Acts 10:34-48; Cf. Psa. 119:172.
       6.   The name to be given (Each prophet); Fulfilled: Acts 11:26.
       7.   Given in God's house (Isa. 56:5); Fulfilled: Acts

11:26 - In the church; Cf. 1 Tim. 3:15.
8. Given by God's mouth (Isa. 56:5; 62:2); Fulfilled: "were called" (Acts 11:26) from "crematizo." Cf. Matt. 2:12, 22; Lk. 2:26; Acts 10:22; Rom. 7:3; 11:4; Heb. 8:5; 11:7; 12:25.
D. Names That Don't Fulfill Prophecy.
1. Hephzibah (Isa. 62:4) "My delight is in her" Deut. 10:15; Cf. 2 King 21:1.
2. Beulah (Isa. 62:4) "Married" - Cf. Jer. 3:14.
3. The holy people (Isa. 62:12) - Cf. Deut. 14:2.
4. The redeemed (Isa. 62:12) - Cf. Ex. 15:13.
5. Sons of God (1 Jno. 3:2) - Cf. Gen. 6:2.
6. Brethren (Acts 6:3) - Cf. Gen. 13:8.
7. Saints (Acts 9:13.) - Cf. Deut. 33:2.
8. Disciples (Acts 21:16) - Cf. Isa. 8:16.
9. Elect (2 Tim. 2:10) - Cf. Isa. 45:4.
E. Name "Christian" Recognized By Inspiration.
1. By Paul - Acts 26:28.
2. By Peter - 1 Peter 4:14-16.
3. By James - Jas. 2:7.

III. **Conclusion.**
A. Must bear image (likeness) and superscription (name) Matt. 22:21.
B. The only name upon which we can unite - others give offense.

Second Conversion Of Peter
Luke 22:32

I. **Introduction.**
A. His case of much interest - so much like many of us.
1. Hasty in speech. Cf. Mt. 16:21-23; Mt. 16:13-16.
2. Hasty in actions - did things on spur of moment. Cf. Mt. 14:24-31; Jno. 13:6-11.
3. Thus in moment of passion, excitment, anger, commit deed he'd regret a lifetime.
4. But whether right or wrong, he was enthusiastic.

II. **Discussion.**
A. His Religious State Prior To Trial of Jesus.
1. Called to discipleship of Jesus. Mt. 4:18-20.
2. Called to apostleship - "greatest work ever given man." Mt. 10:2.
3. But held no official pre-eminence. 2 Cor. 11:5.
4. Especially regarded by the Lord.
a. We would bestow our favors on those nearest us. Cf. Luke 9:28-36.
b. In hour of sorrow, we seek comfort from same. Cf. Mt. 26:36-46.
5. In covenant relationship. John 15:1-9.
6. He had faith. Lk. 22:32.
7. Therefore, he may be called a converted man.
B. The Fall He Experienced.
1. Jesus warned him. Lk. 22:31.
2. Things that led to his fall.
a. Too self-confident. Lk. 22:33; Mk. 14:29-31; Cf. 1 Cor. 10:12.
b. Went to sleep on duty. Mt. 26:36-40.
c. Committed act of rashness. Jno. 18:10.
d. Followed Jesus afar off. Lk. 22:54 - partly back slidden.
e. In bad company - among enemies of Christ. Lk. 22:55.

      f. Denied Christ three times. Lk. 22:56-60.
        (1) Damsel - "know him not." Cf. Mt. 26:69-70.
        (2) With oath to man on porch. Cf. Mt. 26:70-72.
        (3) With cursing and swearing "speech betrayed." Cf. Mt. 26:73-74.
      g. Had Peter thus died, would have been lost. Cf.

C. His Restoration To Divine Favor.
    1. Brought about by means no less remarkable than those that led to his fall.
      a. Cock crew and Lord looked. Lk. 22:60-61.
        (1) No angry word, harsh reproof or humiliating rebuke - just a look - sent conviction to Peter's heart.
        (2) Wept bitterly. V. 61 - all were sad during 3 days - Peter sadder.
      b. Christ arose - "go tell disciples *and Peter*." Mk. 16:7.
      c. His sincerity tested at Sea of Tiberius. Jno. 21.
        (1) They returned to old occupation. v. 3-6.
        (2) "It's the Lord" - Peter jumps overboard. v. 7-14.
        (3) Confessed three times. v. 15-17.

D. His Subsequent Life.
    1. Converts 3,000 on Pentecost. Acts 2; 5,000 in Acts 4.
    2. Work in Lydda (Acts 9:32-35) and Joppa (Acts 9:36-42.)
    3. Then to Gentiles. Acts 10.
    4. His imprisonment and delivery. Acts 12:3-11.
    5. His death. Jno. 21:18-19 - Give tradition of his death.

III. **Conclusion.**
A. Story of mother's picture "Come back" written beneath.
B. Picture of Christ greater - He writes "come back" "*and Peter.*"

Daniel
Daniel 6

I. Introduction.

  A. Written for our learning. Rom. 15:4; 1 Cor. 10:11.

  B. Many examples of courage.

    1. Abraham leaving country (Gen. 12:1-3).

    2. David meeting giant. 1 Sam. 17.

    3. Three in fiery furnace (Dan. 3).

    4. Daniel in lion's den.

  C. My opportunity with theirs - put to shame.

II. Discussion.

  A. Brief History of Daniel.

    1. In Babylonian captivity. Dan. 1:1-7.

    2. Would not defile himself. Dan. 1:8.

    3. Interpreted dream of Nebuchadnezzar. Dan. 2.

      a. Dream forgotten by the king. Dan. 2:5.

      b. Magicians fail to give interpretation. v. 2-11.

      c. Decree to kill wise men. v. 12-13.

      d. Daniel requests time. v. 14-18.

      e. Revealed to Daniel - gives God to glory. vs. 19-30.

    4. Reads handwriting on wall. Dan. 5.

    5. Chosen chief of presidents over 120 princes. Dan. 6:1-3. Didn't weaken faith.

  B. They Became Envious of Daniel's Success. Dan. 6:4.

    1. Worst thing that ever entered human heart.

    2. Began with Satan in Eden. (Milton).

    3. To see another prosper brings into action man's basest passions.

    4. Caused first murder. Gen. 4:1-8.

    5. Example of Joseph. Acts 7:9.

  C. Convention Behind Closed Doors. "Consulted together." v. 7.

    1. These are always hot-beds of heresy.

    2. Could find no fault with Daniel. vs. 4.

3. Must make "law of his God" the means of his fall. v. 5.
4. The Decree. v. 6-9.
   a. King no doubt thought of self glory - couldn't read hearts of these men - signed decree.
   b. Median & Persian law could not be repealed. v. 8.
5. Daniel knew the decree was signed. v. 10.
   a. Prayed on knees three times a day. v. 10.
      (1) Not in secret - but "before open window" vs. 10.
      (2) Not for show of bravery - "as he did aforetime" v. 10.
D. King Discovers His Mistake.
   1. Daniel's enemies report to king. v. 11-13.
   2. King "sore displeased with himself." v. 14.
   3. Endeavored to deliver Daniel. v. 14-15.
E. The Penalty Executed. v. 16.
   1. Impression made on the king. v. 16. "Continual service."
   2. Every note died in palace that night. v. 18.
   3. Arose *early* - went *in haste* to den. v. 19.
   4. Daniel's deliverance. v. 20-23.
   5. His accusers punished. v. 24. Cf. Josephus.
F. Daniel An Example Of Faithfulness. v. 21.
   1. "No hurt upon him" - not because of position, interpreting dreams, etc.
   2. But "because he believed in his God."

III. Conclusion.
A. Though the law has changed, we serve the same God.
B. He requires the same faithfulness of us. Rev. 2:10.

The Christian Platform
Eph. 4:4-6

I. Introduction.
A. Fundamental principles of political party called platform.
B. Each principle called plank in the platform.
C. Christian platform comprises fundamental principles of Christian religion - each principle a plank.

II. Discussion.
A. One God. v. 6.
  1. This the Jehovah of heaven. Cf. 1 Kg. 18:17-40.
  2. This denies atheism (for God is), and also polytheism (for but one God) Cf. 1 Cor. 8:4-6.
  3. Preach "one God" to idol worshipers - call you narrow minded.
  4. Most religions of America believe "one God" - Why? "Bible says so."
B. One Lord - v. 5.
  1. This the one who came to earth, died, arose, ascended. Cf. Acts 2:36.
  2. "Lordship: suggests pre-eminence. Col. 1:18; Eph. 1:20-23.
  3. Proves there is a Lord and but one Lord. Cf. 1. Cor. 8:4-6.
  4. Most religions of América believe "one Lord" - Why? "Bible says so."
C. One Spirit. v. 4.
  1. This the third person of the trinity. 1 Jno. 5:7; Mt. 28:19.
  2. Reproves of sin, righteousness & judgment. Jno. 16:8-11.
  3. There are many false spirits (1 Jno. 4:1) - One true.
  4. Proves there is a spirit and but one true spirit.
  5. Most religions of America believe "one Spirit" - Why? "Bible says so."

D. One Hope. v. 4.
   1. Hope defined: "desire and expectation" Cf. Rom. 8:24-25.
   2. It is an anchor of the soul - Heb. 6:18-19. (Cf. Ingersoll hope.)
   3. Proves there is a hope and but one true hope of gospel.
   4. Most religions of America believe "one hope." — Why? "Bible says so."
E. One Church. vs. 4. Cf. Eph. 1:21-22; Col. 1:18.
   1. Which church? Why not ask, which God, Lord or Spirit?
   2. The one mentioned in Bible. 1 Cor. 1:2; Rom. 16:16.
   3. "If one God" means "but one," why not "one church" but one? Cf. 1 Cor. 12:20.
   4. If believe "one God" because "Bible says so," why not this for same reason?
F. One Faith. v. 5.
   1. Not historical, evangelical and saving faith. Rom. 10:17; John 20:30-31.
   2. Salvation by faith (Heb. 11:6) but not by faith only. (Jas. 2:24).
   3. If "one God" means but one, why not "one faith" mean "but one?"
   4. If believe "one God" because "Bible says so," why not this for same reason?
G. One Baptism. v. 5.
   1. Which?
      a. Water baptism commanded. Acts 10:47-48.
      b. Holy Spirit baptism promises. Acts 1:5.
      c. "Commanded baptism age lasting (Mt. 28:19-20). Again:
      a. Water baptism performed by man. (Acts 8:38-39).
      b. Holy Spirit baptism by Lord (Jno. 1:33).
      c. That performed by man, age lasting (Mt. 28:19-20).
   2. Proper Action. Rom. 6:3-4; Col. 2:12.
   3. Proper subject: Believer who makes proper confession. Acts 8:37; 1 Jno. 2:15; Rom. 10:9-10.
   4. Proper design - remission of sins.
      a. "For remission" part of command in Acts 2:38. Diagram - also 1 Cor. 11:24).
      b. John's baptism "for remission" but not "in name

of Christ" not acceptable. (Acts 19:1-5). Would
reversing it make it so?
5. If believe "one God" because "Bible says so," why
not this?

If A Man Die, Shall He Live Again
Job 14:14

I. Introduction.

    A. Question of interest in all ages - certainty of death makes it so.

    B. To answer the question negatively:

        1. Nothing to God's ultimate glory.

        2. Would be most miserable (1 Cor. 15:19).

    C. To answer affirmatively:

        1. Increase faith & trust in God.

        2. Regulate affections after worldly things.

        3. Support saints in loss of loved ones.

        4. Comfort righteous in death.

    D. Of interest to all classes - saints or sinners.

    E. Resurrection the basic principle of Christianity. 1 Cor. 15:13-18.

II. Discussion.

    A. Proof of A Resurrection.

        1. Types: Isaac; Gen. 22:13; Heb. 11:19; Jonah. Jonah 2:10; Mt. 12:40.

        2. Prophecies: Isa. 26:19; Dan. 12:2; Hos. 13:14.

            a. Other predictions made by them are true. "Babylon" Isa. 13 & 14 ch. Jerusalem. Dan. 9:27; Mt. 24:15.

        3. Demonstrations. 2 Kings 13:21; Jno. 11:44; 1 Cor. 15:12-18.

    B. Will The Body Be Raised?

        1. It is the body that dies. Jas. 2:26; Matt. 10:28.

        2. It is the body that is buried. Mt. 14:12; 27:59-60.

        3. Therefore the body is the thing to be raised.

        4. Bible statements.

            a. The body of Christ arose. Acts 2:27; Lk. 24:3; John 20:27.

            b. "With my dead body shall they arise." Isa. 26:19.

            c. Many bodies of saints arose. Mt. 27:52.

        d. Change our vile bodies. Phil. 3:20-21; Rom. 8:23; 1 Cor. 15:42-44.
    5. Difficulty - Man torn to pieces, devoured, etc.
C. A Universal Resurrection.
    1. Resurrection as broad as death. 1 Cor. 15:22.
        a. Explain "in Christ" and "in Adam."
    2. Resurrection of just and unjust. Acts 24:15; Cf. Mt. 5:45.
    3. All that are in their graves. Jno. 5:28-29.
    4. Death to be destroyed. 1 Cor. 15:26.
        a. Not destroyed as long as one victim remains.
D. One Transaction.
    1. In one hour. Jno. 5:28.
    2. Separation occurs afterwards. Mt. 25:31-32.
    3. John's vision of judgment. Rev. 20:11-12.
    4. Explain 1 Thess. 4:14-16.
E. How Raised?
    1. Not according to nature. Job 14:7-13.
    2. By power of God. 1 Cor. 6:14.
F. When Will It Be?
    1. When Christ comes. 1 Cor. 15:23-25.
    2. At the last day. Jno. 11:24; 1 Cor. 15:52.

III. Conclusion.

A. We will be raised to go to judgment.
B. Our rewards will await us there. Jno. 5:28-29; Dan. 12:2.
C. The resurrection will either be a happy fortune or a sad disaster.

Heartfelt Religion
Jas. 1:27

I. **Introduction.**
   A. Expression not in Bible - Yet idea taught.
   B. We believe in Heartfelt Religion.
   C. All religions are heartfelt.
   D. Every Phase of the subject is misunderstood.

II. **Discussion.**
   A. What Is The Heart? This is misunderstood.
      1. Not the fleshly lobe in side. Psa. 22:26; Eccl. 10:2; Jno. 14:1; Mt. 5:8; Acts 7:54.
      2. Determine by what it does.
         a. Thinks. Gen. 6:5.
         b. Reasons. Mark 2:8.
         c. Understands. Mt. 13:15.
         d. Believes. Rom. 10:10.
         e. Loves. Deut. 6:5.
         f. Desires. Psa. 37:4; Rom. 10:1.
         g. Purposes. Dan. 1:8; 2 Cor. 9:7.
         h. Obeys. Rom. 6:17.
   B. Why Sinner's Heart Needs Changing.
      1. This is misunderstood - not condition of fleshly heart.
      2. Condition of sinner's heart.
         a. Thoughts are evil.
         b. Reasons from human standpoint.
         c. Understanding thus darkened.
         d. Believes a falsehood - false theories, etc.
         e. Loves world and worldly things.
         f. Desires are sensual and devilish.
         g. Purposes are temporal - not eternal.
         h Obeys selfish desires and temporal purposes.
   C. How Is It Changed?
      1. This is misunderstood - not by direct operation.
      2. The Bible plan.

100

a. Thoughts changed by weapons of word. 2 Cor. 10:4; Eph. 6:17.
b. Reasoning changed by testimony. Psa. 19:7.
c. Understanding changed by God's word. Psa. 119:130.
d. Belief changed by word of God. Rom. 10:17.
e. Love changed by Love of God. 1 Jno. 4:19.
f. Desires changed by promises of God. Rev. 22:14.
g. Purposes changed by desire to do right. Prov. 11:23.
h. Obedience changed by love for God. Jno. 14:15.

D. What Is Religion?
  1. This is misunderstood - not something you "get."
  2. But a system of faith and practice. Acts 26:5; Gal. 1:13-14; Jas. 1:26-27. Religion mentioned 5 times in the Bible.

E. What Connection Have Feelings With Christianity?
  1. This is misunderstood - not an evidence of pardon.
  2. Belief of lie will produce same feeling as belief of truth. Gen. 37:23-36.
  3. Hindu mother's religion is heartfelt.
  4. We feel good because we are saved - others think saved because feel good.

III. Conclusion.

A. Conditions to be met.
  1. Faith. Heb. 11:6.
  2. Repentance. Acts 17:30.
  3. Confession. Rom. 10:9-10.
  4. Baptism. Rom. 6:17; 1 Cor. 15:3-4; Rom. 6:3-4.

Heaven
John 14:1-3

I. **Introduction.**
   A. Why speak on the subject?
      1. If you didn't want to go to Calif - not interested in the way.
      2. Must first interest you by a description - so with heaven.
   B. Various figures employed to furnish some conception.
      1. A city. Heb. 11:10; A building. Jno. 14:1-3; A kingdom. Mt. 25:34; A country. Heb. 11:10.
      2. Hence it is not a condition - "prepare *a place* for you."

II. **Discussion.**
   A. Reason For Believing There Is Such A Place.
      1. The Soul of man longs for it.
         a. Universal instinct - Egyptian, Indians - some provision.
         b. Nothing gives so much satisfaction as anticipating "Home of the Soul."
      2. The soul needs such a place.
         a. Satisfaction not attained here. Psa. 17:15; 55:6.
      3. Justice Demands such a place.
         a. Things not right here - man upset whole affair.
         b. Wicked on thrones; saints in dungeons - must be something better for them.
      4. Because Bible says so. Lk. 10:20; Mt. 6:19; 1 Pet. 1:4; Rev. 21:10-27.
   B. A Prepared Place For A Prepared People.
      1. Must follow Jesus. Jno. 12:26; Mt. 7:21; Rev. 22:14; Heb. 5:8-9.
      2. Nothing that defiles can enter. Rev. 21:27.
      3. Promise is to the overcomer. 2 Tim. 2:12; Rev. 2:7.
   C. Attractive Features Of Heaven;
      1. A Holy City.

a. Give John's description as city of gold. Rev. 21:18-21.

b. A place of righteousness - no wicked to trouble. 2 Pet. 3:13; Rev. 21:27; Job 3:1f.

c. Cannot fathom full meaning of "Heaven." Cf. 1 Jno. 3:2.

2. Tree of Life and River of Life. Rev. 22:1-2.

a. First access to tree in Eden. Gen. 3:22-24 - transplanted. Rev. 2:7.

b. River of life clear as crystal - no wonder we'll not hunger nor thirst. Rev. 7:16-17.

3. No Night There. Rev. 21:25.

a. Night's shadows never fall, mantle of night never thrown, tree cast no shadows indicative of setting of sun, sparkling of river never dimmed.

b. No candles, no sun needed. Rev. 21:23; 22:5.

4. No Death There. Rev. 21:4.

a. Cheeks never pale, eyes never set in glassy stare, no crepe on doors, no graves, no death knell, no funeral procession.

b. Describe separation at death - nothing like it there.

5. No Pain There. Rev. 21:4.

6. No weeping there. Rev. 21:4.

a. Earth a vale of tears - man made to mourn.

b. Where Jesus reigns all tears wiped away. Cf. Isa. 35:10.

7. No more curse. Rev. 22:3.

a. Takes us back to Eden - but now end of wandering reached.

b. Curse almost at beginning, but "no more curse" there.

III. Conclusion.

A. Whom I want to meet first in Heaven.

B. His glory in that day.

1. Not a homeless wanderer - but surrounded by palaces.

2. Not a man of sorrows, hated & scorned - but myrids of angels.

3. Not met by few in Galilee - but innumerable host. Rev. 7:9.

The Destiny Of The Wicked
1 Pet. 4:18

I. **Introduction.**
   A. Comment on question of text.
   B. This an age of doubt and speculation - Bible doctrine.
   C. Four prominent answers concerning sinners destiny.
      1. Universal salvation.
      2. No resurrection of unbeliever.
      3. Annihilation.
      4. Endless torment.

II. **Discussion.**
   A. Universal Salvation Theory Investigated.
      1. Arguments used as proof.
         a. "Desire of righteous shall be granted" Prov. 10:24. Reply: Rest of verse.
         b. Attributes of God: Either can and will not, will and cannot, or can and will save all. Reply: The same might be said of present salvation.
      2. The theory disproved. John 8:21; Prov. 11:21; 2 Pet. 2:9.
   B. No Resurrection Theory Investigated.
      1. Arguments used as proof.
         a. To reject Jesus is to reject resurrection. Cf. John 11:25; Reply Jno. 12:48.
         b. "Ungodly shall not stand in judgment." Psa. 1:5. Reply: Cf. 2 Pet. 3:7.
      2. The theory disproved. Jno. 5:28; Acts 24:15; Rev. 1:7; 21:8.
   C. Annihilation Theory Investigated.
      1. Arguments used as proof.
         a. Into smoke consume away. Psa. 37:20. Reply: Cf. v. 19.
         b. Leave neither root nor branch. Mal. 4:1; Reply: "Ashes under feet" v. 3.
         c. Soul to be destroyed. Mt. 10:28; Reply: Luke

15:4; 19:10; Job 19:10; Hosea 4:6; 13:9; Jer. 17:18. (Liddell & S. define: To be wretched or miserable.)

    2. The theory disproved by theory no. 4.

E. Endless Punishment.

    1. Everlasting punishment. Mt. 25:46.

        a. Everlasting from aionios: "without end, never to cease."

        b. Can punishment that ends be everlasting?

        c. Use of word everlasting: Everlasting God (Rom. 16:26); eternal spirit (Heb. 9:14); Eternal savlation. (Heb. 5:8-9); Eternal glory (1 Pet. 5:10); Everlasting life (John 3:16); Everlasting kingdom. (2 Pet. 1:11).

    2. Everlasting fire. Mt. 25:41; 18:8.

    3. Eternal damnation. Mk. 3:29.

    4. Everlasting destruction. 2 Thess. 1:7-9.

    5. Everlasting contempt. Dan. 12:2.

    6. Worse than death without mercy. Heb. 10:28-29.

        a. Can punishment that ends in death be worse than death without mercy?

    7. Hell (gehenna) - fire never quenched - worm dies not.

        a. Gehenna used 12 times in N.T. - always a place of punishment.

    8. Tormented with fire and brimstone. Rev. 14:9-11.

        a. Objection: This "in the presence of Lamb," the other "from the presence," 2 Thess. 1:7-9. Reply: One from God's standpoint, the other from man's.

    9. Tormented day and night forever and ever. Rev. 20:10.

        a. Objection: No day and night in eternity. Reply: Rev. 7:15. Day and night signifies continued service or torment.

    10. After righteous enter city - sinners still without. Rev. 22:14-15.

III. Conclusion.

A. Whosoever not written in book, cast into lake. Rev. 20:15.

B. Will you prepare for the time "when heaven opens her gates"?

C. Or will you go to "abode of rebel angels?"

Liars
Psa. 116:11

I. **Introduction.**
 A. David a little hasty, but no one has monopoly on this commodity.
 B. Cretians especially noted for this quality. Tit. 1:12.
 C. May lock against thief - not so the liar.
 D. Subject not pleasing one, but is a Bible subject. Cf. Gal. 1:10; 2 Tim. 4:3.

II. **Discussion.**
 A. Origin of Lies.
  1. Devil the "father" of them. John 8:44.
  2. Examples of his lies.
   a. In deceiving Eve. Gen. 3:4, 5.
   b. In impugning Job's motives. Job 1:9, 10; 2:4, 5.
   c. Expressing doubt of Christ's divinity. Mt. 4:3.
 B. Kinds of liars.
  1. Common liars. Psa. 50:19.
   a. Lie for purpose of deceiving - exaggerate or manufacture.
   b. Example: Old prophet of Bethel. 1 Kg. 13:11-22.
  2. Jesting liars. Prov. 26:18-19.
  3. Cowardly liars. Isa. 57:11.
   a. Tell lie because afraid to tell the truth.
   b. Examples of cowardly liars.
    (1) Adam & Eve in evading responsibility. Gen. 3:10-13.
    (2) Abraham in calling Sarah his sister. Gen. 20:2-12.
    (3) Parents of blind man. Jno. 9:19-23.
    (4) Peter in denying Christ. Mt. 26:69-74.
  4. Malicious Liars. Psa. 28:3; Jer. 9:8; Prov. 10:18.
   a. Brought about by hatred or spite. Prov. 26:24-25.
   b. Examples of malicious liars.
    (1) Potiphar's wife against Joseph. Gen.

39:14-17.
  (2) Herod to wise men. Mt. 2:8.
5. Commercial Liars.
  a. Lie to obtain money under false pretenses.
  b. Examples of commercial liars.
    (1) Gehazi to Naaman. 2 Kgs. 5:20-27.
    (2) The Roman soldiers. Mt. 28:12-15.
    (3) Ananias and Sapphira. Acts 5:1-10.
6. Social Liars. Prov. 26:28.
  a. Only two classes of social liars - men and women.
  b. Kiss your "despised friend" at door - adore her clothing - then laugh at "silly thing" when gone.
  c. Applaud her children while wishing to club the "little brats."
7. Religious Liars. Rom. 3:4.
  a. Teachers of false doctrines. 1 Tim. 4:1-2; Rom. 1:25.
  b. Those claiming apostolic powers. Rev. 2:2; 2 Cor. 11:13-15.
  c. Those who profess to know Him, but are disobedient. 1 Jno. 2:4; Tit. 1:25.
  d. Those who claim to love God while hating brethren. 1 Jno. 4:20.
  e. Those who claim fellowship with God while in darkness. 1 Jno. 1:6.
C. How God Views Lying.
  1. He hates it. Prov. 6:16-19; 12-22.
  2. Admonishes against it. Eph. 4:25; Col. 3:9; 1 Pet. 3:10.
D. Destiny of Liars. Rev. 21:27; Prov. 19:5; Rev. 21:8.

III. **Conclusion.**
  A. We should abhor lying. Cf. Psa. 119:163.
  B. Even "white lies" should be avoided.
  C. Lies may be acted, as well as spoken.

Sin

I. Introduction.

A. Bible presupposes sin as fact - no effort to demonstrate its reality.

B. Some refuse to admit it - efforts to "explain it away" prove its reality.

C. Sin not a myth, illusion of mind, or creature of imagination.

D. Some may harden themselves - but sin remains.

II. Discussion.

A. Nature of Sin - Defined.
  1. Transgression of law. 1 Jno. 3:4; Rom. 4:15.
      a. Not a "necessity determined by heredity," but free act of creature.
      b. No "original sin." Jer. 31:29-30; Ezek. 18:2-4, 20.
  2. Whatsoever not of faith. Rom. 14:23; Cf. Rom. 10:17.
      a. Examples: Nadab and Abihu. Lev. 10:1-2; Cain, Gen. 4:3-7; Heb. 11:4.
  3. All unrighteousness. 1 Jno. 5:17; Cf. Psa. 119:172.
  4. Thought of foolishness. Prov. 24:9.
      a. May sin in thought as well as deed. Cf. Mt. 5:28.
  5. Omitting known duty. Jas. 4:17.
      a. Sin a "missing of mark," "coming short" Cf. Rom. 3:23; Mt. 23:23.

B. The Origin of Sin.
  1. Philosophers can't explain - Bible explanation reliable.
  2. First appearance among angels, details not given. 2 Pet. 2:4; Jude 6.
  3. Entrance into world fully explained. Rom. 5:12; Gen. 3.

C. The Universality of Sin.
  1. Not merely among uncivilized, but in every land beneath the sun.

108

2. Bible outlines world — embracing character of sin.
   a. Before the flood. Gen. 6:12.
   b. In David's time. Psa. 14:3.
   c. In Isaiah's time. Isa. 53:6.
   d. In Christian era. Rom. 5:12.
   e. The Bible verdict. 1 Kg. 8:46; 1 Jno. 1:8-10; Jas. 3:2.
   f. Only Christ live above it. 1 Pet. 2:22.
D. The Consequences of Sin.
   1. It enslaves. Jno. 8:34. Rom. 6:16; 2 Pet. 2:19.
   2. Separates from God. Isa. 59:2.
   3. Works spiritual death. Gen. 2:16; Rom. 6:23; Jas. 1:15.
   4. Will keep us out of heaven. Jno. 8:21.
   5. Condemns to eternal punishment. 2 Pet. 2:9; Mt. 25:46; 2 Thess. 1:9; Heb. 10:28-29; Rev. 20:10.
   6. Its consequences shown in various incidents.
      a. Flood, destruction of Sodom and Jerusalem, angels cast down to hell, alms houses, penitentiaries.
E. The Remedy For Sin.
   1. Pardonableness of sin, "good news" of gospel. Cf. Acts 3:19; Heb. 8:12.
   2. Christ's blood the great remedy. Heb. 9:22; 1 Jno. 1:7.
      a. He came for this purpose. Isa. 53:6; Jno. 1:29; Tit. 2:14; 1 Jno. 3:5.
   3. He has right to state the conditions.
      a. Faith. Jno. 8:24.
      b. Repentance. Acts 3:19.
      c. Confession. Rom. 10:9-10.
      d. Baptism. Acts 2:38.
      e. Faithfulness. Mt. 24:12-13.

III. Conclusion.
A. Terribleness of sin shown by its cost. Rom. 8:3; 2 Cor. 5:21.
B. Pleasures of sin cannot last. Heb. 11:25.
C. As judgments finds us, we will so remain. Rev. 22:11.

Salvation
Acts 4:12

I. Introduction.
   A. The term implies that there is danger. Mt. 5:22.
   B. It also implies deliverance.
      1.   Israel's deliverance from bondage. Ex. 14:13.
      2.   Our deliverance from sin. Col. 1:13; 1 Thess. 1:10.

II. Discussion.
   A. Imporance of Salvation.
      1.   Salvation from any danger - fire, water, poverty, sickness, death - important.
      2.   Importance shown by its cost. Heb. 9:28.
      3.   Importance shown by limits placed on it. "Only in Christ." Acts 4:12.
      4.   Without salvation we are lost. Lk. 19:10; Jno. 8:21.
      5.   Rescues us from death. Jas. 5:20.
   B. The Elements of Salvation.
      1.   Perfect in Nature.
         a. Law made nothing perfect. Heb. 7:19.
         b. Salvation under it was temporary and partial. Heb. 10:1-4.
         c. The deliverance is complete under the gospel. Heb. 8:12.
      2.   Personal In Application.
         a. Must bear own individual sin. Ezek. 18:20.
         b. Each must account for "himself." 2 Cor. 5:10; Rom 14:12.
         c. Must work out "own salvation." Phil. 2:12; Acts 2:40.
      3.   Present In Obligation.
         a. May be freed from sin this world. Rom. 6:17, 18; 8:2.
         b. Must prepare before Lord returns. Lk. 12:45-47.
         c. Now is day of salvation. 2 Cor. 6:2.
      4.   Free In Bestowal.

        a. A gift of God. Rom. 5:15; 18; Eph. 2:8; Isa. 55:1.

        b. Shall never merit salvation. Lk. 17:10.

    5. Conditional In Reception.

        a. Must do his will. Mt. 7:21; Heb. 5:8-9; Rev. 22:14.

        b. Must "work out" salvation. Phil. 2:12; Acts 10:35.

        c. Must order lives aright. Psa. 50:23.

        d. His conditions:

            (1) Faith. Acts 16:31.

            (2) Repentance. 2 Cor. 7:10.

            (3) Confession. Rom. 10:9-10.

            (4) Baptism. Mk. 16:16; 1 Pet. 3:21.

            (5) Perseverance. Mt. 24:12, 13; Rev. 2:10.

    6. Universal In Provision.

        a. "Whosoever will." Rev. 22:17; Jno. 3:16; Mk. 16:15.

        b. Christ died for all. Heb. 2:9; 1 Jno. 2:2.

        c. Able and willing to save all. Heb. 7:25; 1 Tim. 2:3-4.

        d. A common salvation. Jude 3.

    7. Great In Value.

        a. Called "great salvation." Heb. 2:3.

        b. Other salvations great - Noah, Israel, Daniel - none like this.

        c. Its greatness emphasized by torture of hell. Heb. 10:28, 29; Rev. 14:9-11.

        d. Also by bliss of heaven. Rev. 21:4.

    8. Eternal In Duration.

        a. Other salvations were temporal. Noah, Isreal.

        b. But this one is eternal. Heb. 5:8-9; 2 Tim. 2:10; 1 Jno. 2:25.

III. Conclusion.

A. No man can be saved who rejects. Jno. 5:40; 12:48.

B. Neither those who neglect. Heb. 2:3.

Will A Man Rob God?
Mal. 3:8-10

I. Introduction.
  A. Robber defined.
    1. One who takes something by force; condition to-day.
    2. One who steals - the thief is as much robber as the other.
    3. One who defrauds or cheats - we patronize such.
    4. One who withholds that which belongs to another.
    5. We cannot rob God like the first definition. (Mt. 6:19-20), but can all the others.
  2. Comment on text - "strange charge."

II. Discussion.
  A. Ways In Which We May Rob God.
    1. Stealing His words from others. Jer. 23:25-32.
      a. By substituting dreams.
      b. By substituting creeds. Cf. 2 Tim. 3:16-17.
      c. By failing to warn others. Ezek. 3:17-21.
      d. By failing to teach duties, on giving, etc.
    2. Withholding Honor as Creator - Evolution.
    3. Withholding our service.
      a. We are not our own. 1 Cor. 6:19-21.
      b. Should give ourselves to Him. 2 Cor. 8:5.
      c. Should not hide our talent. Matt. 25:24-30.
      d. Cf. Sunday night services, etc.
    4. Withholding Gratitude.
      a. Should give thanks for all his blessings - "in deeds as well as words".
    5. By defrauding the Poor.
      a. God condemns such = Mal. 3:5; Jas. 5:4; 1 Thess. 4:6.
      b. As we treat our brethren we treat the Lord. Mt. 25:35-45; 1 Jno. 3:17.
    6. Withholding our means.

a. What we have really belongs to God. 1 Cor. 10:26; Ezek. 16:17.

b. We are stewards (1 Pet. 4:10) having charge of another's possessions.

   (1) Must be faithful. 1 Cor. 4:2.

   (2) Must not waste goods. Lk. 16:1.

   (3) Allowed to provide for honest things 2 Cor. 8:21 - but must not spend Lord's part on pleasures.

   (4) Should seek kingdom of God first. Mt. 6:33; Not leave Lord's business till the last.

   (5) David said all they gave for house of God already His. 1 Chron. 29:14-16.

c. Must give according to our means. 2 Cor. 8:12; 1 Cor. 16:1-2.

d. We reap what we sow. Gal. 6:7-8; 2 Cor. 9:6.

   (1) First scandal in church over a financial matter. Acts 5.

e. Covetous man very unlike Christ.

   (1) Christ gave all.

   (2) Covetous man like a "sponge."

f. Send your treasures on before. Mt. 6:19.

g. If we purpose, God will make us able. 2 Cor. 9:7-10.

III. Conclusion.

A. When we rob God we fatally rob ourselves.

B. Ill. Dying millionaire sends for preacher to read Bible - opened at Mt. 6:19-20; Lk. 16:19-31; 1 Tim. 6:17. Read all - "Why haven't you told me these things before?"

The Star In The East
Mt. 2:1-13

I. **Introduction.**
    A. Wise men come from east - star west of them. v. 1.
    B. Somehow they knew by this star that Christ was born. v. 2.
    C. Their inquiry troubled Herod - asked where his birth to be. v. 3-6.

II. **Discussion.**
    A. Origin of Christmas.
       1. Dec. 21 shortest day - light begins to lengthen on Dec. 25 - regarded as birthday of sun-god and festival celebrated by heathen.
       2. Chrysostom says: "On this day, also, the birthday of Christ was lately fixed at Rome.'
    B. Not The Birthday of Christ.
       1. His birthday cannot be ascertained by N.T. or any other source.
       2. If it were His birthday, no time to act as men do - rowdyism, etc.
       3. Immaterial whether this the date - two memorials. Rom. 6:3-4; 1 Cor. 11.
       4. But 'tis fitting to recall with gratitude the fact of his birth - great event.
       5. No sin to observe it with thanksgiving (Isa. 9:6-7), but sin to observe it as consecrated to God.
       6. Should manifest spirit of Christ by "golden rule." Mt. 7:12.
       7. Should be proud of religion of Christ - Only one I ever heard of that people were ashamed of. Cf. 1 Pet. 4:16; Lk. 9:26.
    C. What Beneath The Star? v. 9.
       1. A Visible token of God's Love. Jno. 3:16; Rom. 5:8; 1 Jno. 4:9.
         a. We should love him back. 1 Jno. 4:19; 5:3; Jno.

14:15.
2. Hope For a Lost World. Cf. Eph. 2:12; 1 Thess. 4:13.
   a. Loss of hope man's greatest loss. Property, friends, etc.
   b. Hope gives us strong consolation. Heb. 6:18-19; 1 Cor. 13:13.
   c. Babe of Nile the hope of Israel - Babe of Bethlehem hope of world.
3. A great demonstration of unselfishness. Mt. 20:28.
   a. We are failures unless we serve others. Mt. 20:27; Jas. 4:3.
4. The light of the world. Jno. 8:12.
5. "Immanuel" - God with us. Mt. 1:23; Jno. 1:14; 1 Tim. 3:16.
   a. Picture of aurora on ceiling studied with difficulty - if reflected in mirror, with ease.
   b. God in unapproachable light. 1 Tim. 6:16; Christ the mirror. Jno. 14:9; Heb. 1:3.
6. The world's great leader - must follow guide. 1 Pet. 2:21; Mt. 10:28.
7. A friend of sinners. Mt. 11:19.
8. The world's Redeemer. Isa. 59:20.
D. What The Wise Men Did.
   1. Gave precious gifts. v. 11.
   2. Best thing they gave was their hearts. v. 11.
   3. The same should be our offering. 2 Cor. 8:5.
      a. "No gift is so precious to him as our love."

III. Conclusion.
A. Three strange things.
   1. That all do not follow him - ruin or happiness.
   2. That some who follow, follow afar off - indifference.
   3. That any who ever followed would forsake him - friend for enemy.

Resolutions
Luke 16:4

I. **Introduction.**
   A. Should take retrospective view as we face a new year.
   B. Need something to make us "remember our faults." Cf. Gen. 41:9.
   C. Business firm should take inventory - so should Christians.
   D. If we never purpose we never accomplish.
   E. But resolutions for good should not be broken. Cf. Eccl. 5:4-5.

II. **Discussion.**
   A. Bible upholds resolving or purposing.
      1. God himself purposed. Isa. 14:24-27; Eph. 3:10-11.
      2. Daniel purposed in heart. Dan. 1:8.
      3. Paul often purposed. Acts 19:21; Rom. 1:13; Phil. 3:13-14.
      4. Others exhorted to purpose. 2 Cor. 9:7.
   B. Low Aim Is A Crime.
      1. Not bound to succeed, but bound to aim high - "wagon to star."
      2. If we expect to do "big things" must plan "big things" - tent meetings, etc.
      3. Make good beginning - "well begun is half done."
      4. If we fail, let us fail after we try.
   C. Some Resolutions worth making.
      1. To be more faithful in Church attendance.
         a. Should not forsake the assembly. Heb. 10:25.
         b. To neglect is a serious thing. Heb. 2:2, 3; 10:28-29; John 6:53.
         c. Should not let earthly friends (company) lead us from heavenly friend. Mt. 18:20; 10:37.
         d. If ox gets habit of falling in pit, fill the pit or sell the ox.
         e. Faithful & liberal in giving. 1 Cor. 16:1-2; 2 Cor.

9:6-7.
2. To Be more humble and unselfish.
   a. Don't erect idol called self and want others to.
   b. Admonitions against pride and selfishness. Prov. 16:18; Jas. 4:6; Rom. 12:3.
   c. The secret of true greatness. Mt. 18:1-4; 20:27f.

3. To be more prayerful.
   a. God is willing to listen. 1 Pet. 3:12.
   b. He has promised to answer. Mt. 7:9-11; 1 Jno. 5:15.
   c. And has commanded us to pray. 1 Tim. 2:8; Mt. 6:5-6.
   d. Some thoughts on prayer.
      (1) Prayer may cause us to quit sinning - sin will cause us to quit praying.
      (2) Trouble drives us to prayer - prayer drives away trouble.
      (3) We should pray without ceasing (1 Thess. 5:17). Some cease without praying.

4. To assist the unfortunate.
   a. Hundred hearts worse bruised than mine - help.
   b. Imbibe spirit of Christ (Jno. 5:1-8; Lk. 7:11-17; Rom. 12:15; Jno. 11:35.
      (1) Sorrows humanize the race and tears are showers that fertilize world.

5. To make closer study of Bible.
   a. Lack of Bible information appalling. "Man reciting Lord's prayer."
   b. Ill. preacher held up hand that he had read 17th chapter of Mark.
   c. How many can quote and locate 3 verses in the Bible.
   d. Close study reveals things "Help meet" and Rom.
      14:20 (Bible classes).

6. If not Christian, resolve to be.
   a. "Road to hell paved with good intentions."
   b. Deciding point must be reached sometime. Cf. Josh. 24:15.

D. What We Do, Do Earnestly.
   1. People do evil this way. Mich. 7:3.
   2. This should govern the righteous. Jas. 5:17; Heb. 2:1; Jude 3.

III. Conclusion.

A. This new year will be inscribed on many monuments.

B. Plan as though we'd live forever; live as though we'd die today.

Believing A Lie
2 Thess. 2:10-12

I. Introduction.
    A. Two great weaknesses of man.
        1. Reliable otherwise often unreliable in handling word of God.
        2. Most people believe man's story before they will Christ. (Modern conversions)
    B. The popular view: "It makes no difference."
        1. Nature strikes those who violate her laws regardless of their good faith.
    C. Often warn against being liar, seldom warn against believing one.

II. Discussion.
    A. False Testimony Affects Mind Same As Truth. Gen. 37:31-36.
        1. Reports of persons killed during war often false.
    B. Acceptance of Falsehood Unfits Mind For Reception of Truth.
        1. Jacob could hardly believe Joseph alive. Gen. 45:25-28.
        2. Easier to teach child who has not learned than one who learned wrongly. (Religion)
    C. Different Faiths Make Different Denominations.
        1. Pharisees and Sadducees. Mt. 16:6-12; Acts 23:6-8.
        2. If right for 50 men to preach 50 conflicting doctrines, right for one (elaborate).
        3. Good opportunity lost to establish Jew & Gentile denominations. Acts 15; Gal. 1:8. 9.
        4. And three more at Corinth. 1 Cor. 1:11-13.
        5. Lord must be the builder. Psa. 127:1.
        6. Other plants to be rooted up. Mt. 15:13.
    D. Evidence That It Makes A Difference.
        1. It is the truth that makes free. Jno. 8:32.
        2. The blind leading the blind. Mt. 15:14.

3. False prophets and their followers alike condemned. Jer. 14:12-16.
4. Warning against false prophets. Mt. 7:15-23.
5. Warning against doctrines of men. Mt. 15:1-9.
    a. If right to believe anything, right to teach anything.
    b. Unjust to condemn man for preaching something that will save men. Cf. Gal. 1:8.
6. Paul's instruction to Timothy. 1 Tim. 4:1-2; 2 Tim 2:5.
    a. Also Titus. Tit. 1:10-11.
7. Peter's instruction - "pernicious ways." 2 Pet. 2:1-2.
8. John's testimony. "bidding God's speed." 2 Jno. 11.

E. Examples of Misdirected Faith.
1. Adam and Eve. Gen. 3 - result to world.
2. Respecting the flood. Gen. 6; 2 Pet. 2:5.
3. Spies false report. Num. 13:25-33; 14:1-45.
4. Old prophet's lie. 1 Kg. 13.

F. Jesus The Way.
1. We must enter by him. Jno. 14:6; 10:9; 10:1.
2. Two roads. Mt. 7:13, 14 - Does it matter which we take?
3. Salvation in Christ only. Acts 4:11-12.

G. Sincerity Not Sufficient.
1. Man's ways may seem right to him. Prov. 12:15; 16:2.
2. Seeming right don't make them so. Prov. 14:12.
3. Church at Laodicea thought they were right. Rev. 3:17.
4. Saul was honest. Acts 23:1.
5. Believing a lie leads to condemnation (text.)

III. Conclusion.
A. Three things led to strong delusion.
1. Loved not the truth. v. 10.*
2. Believed not the truth. v. 12.
3. Had pleasure in unrighteousness. v. 12.

B. Reverse the matter and salvation results.

Secret Discipleship
John 19:38

I. **Introduction.**
   A. In many respects secrets are hard to keep.
   B. Easier to keep discipleship secret than most other things.
   C. Joseph no worse than many others of that secret gang today.
   D. Ill. Girl in school who kept religion a secret.
   E. Ill. Little girl found mother's religion in trunk.

II. **Discussion.**
   A. Points Concerning Joseph.
   1. An honorable counsellor (Jewish Sanhedrim) Mk. 15:43.
   2. A good and just man. Lk. 23:50.
   3. Did not consent to crucifixion. Lk. 23:51.
      a. We can't be saved on what we don't do.
   4. Waited for kingdom of God. Lk. 23:51.
   5. Yet he was a secret disciple. Jno. 19:38.
   6. Went boldly to Pilate - declared himself. Mk. 15:43.
   7. Did what others failed to do - buried Jesus. Mt. 27:60.
      a. Better late than never - this an age-lasting memorial to Joseph.
   B. Hiding Our Light.
   1. Christians are light of world. Mt. 5:14; Phil. 2:15.
   2. Must not hide our light. Mt. 5:15; Lk. 11:33.
   3. Two sides to Christianity - secret and manifest.
   4. Things we may do secretly.
      a. Giving alms. Mt. 6:1-4. But these may be revealed. Acts 9:36; 10:2.
      b. Prayer. Mt. 6:5-6 - but circumstances may be such that secret prayer would be hiding light. Cf. Dan. 6:10.
   5. Things we must do openly.

a. Stand up for the gospel. Jude 3. If Christ assailed, take his part.
b. Engage in pure speech. Eph. 4:29; 5:4; Tit. 2:8.
c. Various works of righteousness. Mt. 5:16; Jas. 2:18; 3:13; 1 Pet. 2:12.
   (1) Consider one another respecting assembly. Heb. 10:24, 25.
   (2) Kindness and hospitality. Eph. 4:32; 1 Pet. 4:9-10.
   (3) Love. 1 Jno. 3:17-18. Cf. Prov. 27:5.
C. Some Secrets of Secret Discipleship.
   1. Cowardice. Jno. 19:38; Cf. Jno. 9:22; 7:13.
      a. Many have had courage to die martyrs.
      b. Should not fear man. Mt. 10:28; Heb. 13:6.
      c. Many who are disciples openly might have been disciples secretly, had they lived in Joseph's day.
   2. Ashamed to acknowledge it.
      a. God not ashamed to be called our God. Heb. 11:16.
      b. Christ not ashamed to call us brethren. Heb. 2:11.
      c. Paul not ashamed of it. Rom. 1:16; 2 Tim. 1:12.
      d. We are admonished not to be ashamed. 1 Pet. 4:16; 2 Tim. 1:8.
      e. If we are, Christ will be ashamed of us. Mk. 8:38.
   3. Desire for popularity. Cf. Jno. 12:42-43.
      a. Friendship of world enmity with God. Jas. 4:4; Luke 16:15.
      b. Should not seek to please men. Gal. 1:10; 1 Thess. 2:4.

III. Conclusion.
A. No such thing as "making up for lost time."
B. We may regret it and receive pardon.
C. Bold disciples needed in world today.

Preaching Christ
2 Cor. 4:5

I. **Introduction.**

    A. It pleased God by foolishness of preaching to save 1 Cor. 1:21.

    B. Some men proclaim themselves. Prov. 20:6; 2 Cor. 4:5.

    C. Some preach doctrines of men. Mt. 15:9.

    D. Once Moses was preached. Acts 15:21.

    E. But Christ the apostles' theme. Acts 8:5; 1 Cor. 2:2.

II. **Discussion.**

    A. How To Preach Christ.

        1. The Eternity of His existence.

           a. Was before creation. Jno. 1:1, 2; 17:5; Col. 1:17.

           b. From everlasting. Micah 5:2.

           c. Will continue forever. Heb. 1:10-12; 13:8.

        2. The Purity of His Nature.

           a. He knew no sin. 2 Cor. 5:21; 1 Pet. 2:22.

           b. Holy, harmless, undefiled. Heb. 7:26.

        3. The Depth of His Humiliation.

           a. From heaven to manger. Luke 2:7.

           b. From riches to poverty. 2 Cor. 8:9; Mt. 8:20.

           c. From Deity to lowest of humanity. Phil. 2:6-7.

        4. The Wisdom of His Teaching.

           a. Astonished people at Jerusalem. Luke 2:47.

           b. Never man so spake. Jno. 7:46; Mt. 13:54.

        5. The Excellent of His Obedience.

           a. He came to obey God's will. Heb. 10:7; Lk. 2:42; Jno. 8:29.

           b. Obedient even to death. Phil. 2:8.

        6. The Perfection of His Example.

           a. Made perfect through suffering. Heb. 2:10; 5:8-9.

           b. Became our example. 1 Pet. 2:21.

        7. The Splendor of His Miracles.

           a. Healed the sick. Mt. 4:23.

       b. Stilled the tempest. Mt. 8:23-27.
       c. Raised the dead. Jno. 11:43-44.
  8. The Extent of His Suffering.
       a. Suffered shame. Stripped of clothes. Heb. 12:2;
          Jno. 19:23-24.
       b. The tortures of crucifixion.
  9. The Efficacy of His Death.
       a. Wrought reconciliation. Rom. 5:9-10.
       b. Redeemed from sin. Eph. 1:7; 1 Pet. 1:18-19.
10. The Power of His Resurrection.
       a. Death could not hold him. Acts 2:24; Phil. 3:10.
       b. Made ours possible. 1 Cor. 15:12.
11. The Glory of His Ascension.
       a. Ascended with clouds. Acts 1:9-10.
       b. Received up into glory. 1 Tim. 3:16; Jno. 7:39.
12. The Sufficiency of His Plan.
       a. Has given all things needed. 2 Tim. 3:16-17; 2
          Pet. 1:3.
13. The Supremacy of His Reign.
       a. Claimed all authority. Mt. 28:18.
       b. Exalted above all. Phil. 2:9; Eph. 1:20-22; Col.
          1:18.
14. The Certainty of His Coming.
       a. Every eye shall see him. Rev. 1:7.
15. The Righteousness of His Judgment.
       a. Called righteous judge. 2 Tim. 4:8.
       b. Righteous because each receives his deserts.
          Acts 17:30; 2 Cor. 5:10.
16. The Horrors of His Condemnation.
       a. Eternal separation from God. 2 Thess. 1:8-9.
       b. An everlasting fire. Mt. 26:41; Rev. 14:9-11.
17. The Bliss of His Reward.
       a. Great reward in heaven. Mt. 5:12; 1 Pet. 1:4.
       b. All sorrow ended. Rev. 21:4.

III. Conclusion.
  A. These are wonderful things concerning Christ.
  B. We must obey to be benefited by them. Heb. 5:8-9.

Take Away The Stone
John 11:39

I. **Introduction.**

   A. Relate the story of sickness and death of Lazarus. v. 1-37.

   B. At grave Jesus said, "take away the stone." v. 39.

   C. When he arose, Jesus said, "Loose him and let him go."

II. **Discussion.**

   A. The Reason For These Requirements.

      1. Why did not Jesus remove the stone?

         a. He could have removed it by physical power or power of word.

         b. He could have raised Lazarus without moving the stone.

      2. Why did not Jesus loose him?

         a. He could have done this as easily as they.

         b. The power that raised him could have loosed him.

      3. But he required them to do what they could.

   B. God Never Does What Man Can Do For Himself.

      1. Salvation in ark. Gen. 6 - Noah required to "build."

      2. Deliverance of Israel.

         a. He chose Moses "bring them out." Ex. 3:7-10.

         b. Required Moses to use the rod at the sea. Ex. 14:15-26.

      3. Removing plaque of serpents.

         a. Moses required to "make brazen serpent." Num. 21:8, 9.

         b. Israel required to "look." v. 8, 9.

      4. Naaman required to "dip." 2 Kgs. 5:10.

      5. Blind man required to "wash." Jno. 9:7.

   C. God Always Does What Man Cannot Do.

      1. Note what God did in each of the previous examples.

      2. The same is true in saving people in this age.

a. He furnished the sacrifice. Heb. 10:4; 9:22; Rom. 5:6.
b. He gave the plan. Jer. 10:23; Gal. 1:11; 2 Tim. 1:9; Tit. 3:5.
c. He gives the salvation. Eph. 2:8, 9.
d. He enrolls our names in heaven. Rev. 3:5.
e. He prepares the home for us. Jno. 14:1-3.
D. Some Stones We Must Roll Away.
1. To The Sinner.
a. The stone of unbelief. Jno. 8:24; Acts 16:31;
b. The stone of impenitence. Rom. 2:5; Acts 17:30-31.
c. The stone of Denial. Mt. 10:32-33; Rom. 10:9-10.
d. The stone of Disobedience. Eph. 5:6; Rom. 6:17, 18.
2. To the child of God.
a. The stone of indifference. Rom. 12:11; Heb. 6:12; Eccl. 9:10.
b. The stone of partiality. Jas. 2:1-4; 1 Tim. 5:21.
c. The stone of ignorance. 2 Pet. 3:18; 2 Tim. 2:15.
d. The stone of love for world. Rom. 12:1-2; 1 Jno. 2:15-17; Mt. 16:24.
e. The stone of Carnality. 1 Cor. 3:3; Rom. 8:6, 7.
f. The stone of malice. 1 Pet. 2:1.
g. The stone of self-esteem. Rom. 12:3; Gal. 6:3.
h. The stone of stinginess. 2 Cor. 9:6-8.

III. **Conclusion.**
A. Some expect God to do it all - wait for the Spirit to accomplish.
B. Others depend on the decree of God.
C. God wants all to be saved. 1 Tim. 2:4; 2 Pet. 3:9.
D. But salvation is conditional - man must act for himself. Mt. 7:21; Heb. 5:8-9; Rev. 22:14.

The Kingdom Of Satan
Mt. 12:26

I. **Introduction.**
   A. The devil has a kingdom as shown by the text.
   B. He does not oppose himself. Mt. 12:25.
   C. His works may be carried on in a seemingly contradictory way.
   D. But these all harmonize so long as God is opposed.

II. **Discussion.**
   A. The King Himself.
      1. His various names.
         a. "King whose name is Apollyon (Destroyer)." Rev. 9:11.
         b. Beelzebub the prince of devils. Mt. 12:24.
         c. Called Belial (worthlessness). 2 Cor. 6:15.
         d. Referred to as the Devil (slanderer). Mt. 4:1.
         e. Also called Satan (adversary). Lk. 22:31.
      2. His Character.
         a. Sinned from the beginning. 1 Jno. 3:8.
         b. He tempts people to sin. Mt. 4:3; 1 Thess. 3:5.
         c. He practices deception. 2 Cor. 11:3, 14.
         d. He is a murderer and liar. Jno. 8:44.
         e. The adversary of man. 1 Pet. 5:8.
      3. A Personal Being.
         a. This shown by his names and characteristics.
         b. He disputed with Michael. Jude 9.
   B. His Dominion.
      1. Various expressions show his dominion.
         a. The prince of this world. Jno. 12:31.
         b. Prince of the power of the air. Eph. 2:2.
         c. Claimed dominion of whole world. Lk. 4:6, 7.
      2. His Subjects.
         a. The whole world in wickedness. 1 Jno. 5:19.
         b. His subjects are in bondage. Jno. 8:34; 2 Tim. 2:26; 2 Pet. 2:19.

c. They serve him by choice. Josh. 24:15; Jno. 5:40.

d. How he holds his subjects.

    (1) By the pleasures of sin. 2 Tim. 3:4; Heb. 11:25.

    (2) Blinds them to the truth. 2 Cor. 4:4.

    (3) Snatches word from their hearts. Luke 8:12.

C. His System of Religion - Meets Desire For Worship.

    1. Called the "god of the world." 2 Cor. 4:4.

    2. He has a synagogue. Rev. 2:9.

    3. He has ministers. 2 Cor. 11:15.

    4. He has doctrines to be preached. 1 Tim. 4:1-2.

      a. Promulgated by "seducing spirits." Cf. Deut. 18:10-11.

      b. We may do what God says not to do. Gen. 3:1-5.

      c. Not necessary to do what God says. (elaborate)

      d. No hell to be avoided. Cf. Mt. 25:41.

      e. You'll get another chance anyway. Cf. Mt. 25:41.

    5. He has sacrifices (Idolatrous worship). 1 Cor. 10:20; Deut. 32:17.

    6. He has a "cup" and "table." 1 Cor. 10:21; Deut. 32:38.

D. Deliverance Through Calvary.

    1. Purpose of Christianity to destroy devil's works. Rom. 16:20; Heb. 2:10; 1 Jno. 3:8.

    2. Deliverance effected by the blood. Col. 1:13, 14.

    3. The plan of deliverance.

      a. Faith. Jno. 8:24.

      b. Repentance. Luke 13:3.

      c. Confession. Mt. 10:32.

      d. Baptism. Acts 2:38.

III. Conclusion.

A. To remain in his kingdom insures punishment. Mt. 25:41.

B. If we serve him here we'll dwell with him hereafter. Rev. 14:9-11; 20:10.

Christ Our Example
1 Pet. 2:21

I. **Introduction.**
   A. We are creatures of imitation - example needed.
   B. No man can be followed without limitations. 1 Cor. 11:1.
   C. Word "example" means "copy" or "pattern."
   D. Ill. Teacher writes a "copy" for pupil - try to imitate it.

II. **Discussion.**
   A. The Value of Examples.
      1. They simplify the nature of our duties - as concrete to abstract.
      2. Precepts tell us our duty - examples show it possible.
      3. Examples urge us to imitation. Rom. 11:14.
   B. A Perfect Example.
      1. We like a perfect pattern for any undertaking.
      2. Wouldn't want to depend entirely on imperfect in Christianity.
      3. Christ is a perfect copy.
        a. He did no sin. 1 Pet. 2:22; Isa. 53:9; 2 Cor. 5:21.
        b. Made perfect through suffering. Heb. 2:10.
   C. Must Imitate Him.
      1. No man ever surpassed or equaled Him. 1 Kg. 8:46; Eccl. 7:20; 1 Jno. 1:8-10.
      2. If so he would be as good a pattern as Christ.
      3. The nearer we imitate fhe copy the better we look.
        a. Must stay in His company to look and act like him.
        b. Some look and act like devil because they run with him. 1 Cor. 15:33.
   D. In What Is He Our Example?
      1. In Suffering.
        a. In this we should follow Him. 1 Pet. 2:21; 4:1; Heb. 5:8, 9; Rev. 2:10.

129

   b. An honor to suffer for him. Acts 5:41; 1 Pet. 3:14; 4:16.

   c. If we follow Him we will suffer. 2 Tim. 3:12.

  2. In Service.

   a. He came to serve others Mt. 20:28; Lk. 22:27.

   b. We must serve others. Mk. 10:35-44.

   c. Bear each other's burdens. Gal. 6:2; Rom. 15:1; 1 Cor. 12:25, 26.

  3. In Love.

   a. Loved us so much He gave Himself (Generosity). Eph. 5:12.

   b. We should love him likewise. 1 Jno. 4:19; 2 Cor. 8:5.

   c. Should love each other to this extent. Jno. 13:34; 1 Jno. 3:16.

  4. In Patience.

   a. He was meek and lowly. Mt. 11:28, 29.

   b. When persecuted, opened not His mouth. Isa. 53:7; Mark 15:3-5; Heb. 12:3; 1 Pet. 2:23.

   c. We must act likewise. Eph. 4:2; 1 Pet. 2:20.

  5. In Forgiveness.

   a. Prayed for forgiveness of His murderers. Luke 23:34.

   b. We must imitate Him. Mt. 6:14, 15; Col. 3:13; Acts 7:60.

  6. In Self-Renunciation.

   a. Sought not His own pleasure. Rom. 15:2-3.

   b. We must seek the welfare of others. Rom. 15:5-7; Phil. 2:4, 5.

   c. Renounced riches of heaven. 2 Cor. 8:9.

   d. We should be willing to renounce riches for his sake. Heb. 11:24-26.

  7. In Obedience.

   a. Obedient to His parents. Luke 2:51.

   b. Obedient to heavenly Father. Jno. 6:38; 8:29.

   c. We should walk as He walked. 1 Jno. 2:6.

III. Conclusion.

 A. A glorious thing to be a Christian - but wonderful responsibilities involved.

 B. Christ's example blessing to us to the extent we strive to imitate it.

 C. The glorious reward makes it worth the effort.

The Precious Promises
2 Pet. 1:4

I. Introduction.

    A. Promises easily made but easier broken.

    B. We should endeavor to carry out our promises.

    C. Should be careful not to make rash promises. Cf. Judg. 11:30-31; Mt. 14:7.

    D. God's promises are exceeding great and precious. Text.

II. Discussion.

    A. Two Classes of Promises.

        1. Unconditional promises.

            a. Seedtime and harvest, etc. Gen. 8:22.

            b. No more world-destruction by flood. Gen. 9:11.

            c. The promise of a Redeemer. Gen. 3:15; Acts 13:23.

            d. A future world-destruction. 2 Pet. 3:6-10.

            e. Second coming of Christ. Acts 1:9-11.

            f. The general resurrection. 1 Cor. 15:21, 22; Jno. 5:28, 29.

        2. Conditional Promises.

            a. Remission of sins. Jer. 31:24; Cf. Acts 10:43; 2:38.

                (1) Preciousness shown by its cost. Heb. 9:22.

            b. Answer to prayer. Mt. 7:11; Cf. Jas. 1:6, 7; 1 Jno. 3:22; 5:14.

            c. All things work for our good. Rom. 8:28.

            d. All spiritual blessings. Eph. 1:3; 2 Cor. 1:20.

            e. The glorious resurrection. Rom. 8:11; Phil. 3:11; Luke 20:35; Heb. 11:35.

            f. The everlasting kingdom. Jas. 2:5; Mt. 25:34.

            g. Eternal Life. 1 Jno. 2:25; 1 Tim. 4:8; Heb. 10:35-36; Jas. 1:12.

    B. Do God's Promises Ever Fail?

        1. Unconditional promises never fail. Num. 23:19.

a. Apply to unconditional promises previously mentioned.
2. Conditional promises fail if conditions not met.
   a. Blessing or cursing depends on man's acts. Deut. 28:1-2, 15.
   b. Will repent of promised good. Jer. 18:9-10.
   c. "You shall know my breach of promise." Num. 14:34.
   d. Apply to conditional promises previously mentioned.
3. Conditional promises never fail if conditions met.
   a. One word of all He promised did not fail. 1 Kg. 8:56.
   b. He is faithful that promised. Heb. 10:23.
   c. Not slack concerning His promises. 2 Pet. 3:9.
   d. Apply to conditional promises previously mentioned.
C. Delayed Fulfillment No Proof of Failure.
   1. Some set hearts to do evil because sentence not speedily executed. Eccl. 8:11.
   2. "Where the promise of His coming?" 2 Pet. 3:4.
   3. A thousand years as one day. 2 Pet. 3:8.
   4. Promised destruction by flood delayed a century.
   5. Promise to Abraham 2000 years before fulfilled. Gen. 12:3; Gal. 3:16.

III. Conclusion.
A. Value of these promises should move us to obedience.
B. We cannot now fathom their full meaning. 1 Jno. 3:2.
C. To reject promises of God is a sad mistake.

Justifying Self
Job 9:20

I. **Introduction.**
   A. All sin is condemned by the Lord.
   B. Every justification for sin is a condemnation of God. Job 40:8.
   C. Terrible to abuse God and then justify self for it.
   D. But man is prone to justify self.

II. **Discussion.**
   A. Points Respecting Job.
      1. He was perfect and upright. Job. 1:8.
      2. He was sorely afflicted at the instigation of Satan. Job. 1:10-11.
      3. His three friends came to tantalize him.
      4. He admitted that self-justification was condemnation - Text.
      5. Yet this was his outstanding fault. Job 32:2; 34:5.
   B. Other Examples of Self-Justification.
      1. Adam and Eve for their sin.
         a. Adam said it was the woman's fault - or God's fault. Gen. 3:12.
         b. Eve said the serpent was to blame. Gen. 3:13.
      2. Saul for His transgression. 1 Sam. 15.
         a. The people spared the best for sacrifice. v. 15.
         b. He actually insisted he had obeyed. v. 19-20.
         c. God's condemnation. v. 22-23.
      3. The Lawyer. Lk. 10:25-37.
         a. Note how he was forced to answer own question. v. 25-27.
         b. Endeavored to justify self by changing subjects. v. 29
      4. The Pharisees. Luke 16:14-15.
         a. Would take any position to justify self. Mt. 21:25-27.
         b. The Pharisee's reference to the publican. Lk.

18:10-12.
5. Some will justify self at judgment.
    a. Will claim many works to their credit. Mt. 7:22-23.
    b. Will urge ignorance for their failure. Mt. 25:41f.
C. Three Reasons For Self-Justification.
    1. To satisfy own conscience.
        a. Filthy generation pure in own eyes. Prov. 30:12.
        b. Church at Laodicea was self-satisifed. Rev. 3:17.
    2. To receive man's approbation.
        a. This was true of Pharisees. Lk. 16:14-15.
        b. They desired to appear righteous unto men. Mt. 23:27-28.
    3. To avoid God's condemnation.
        a. This was true of Adam, Eve and Saul and will be of those at the judgment.
D. Present Day Efforts at Self-Justification.
    1. Infidelity is often a self-justification for sin.
    2. Religious division used by some as excuse for rejecting Bible.
    3. "What is to be will be" used by some to excuse their sins.
    4. Some are "waiting God's own time."
    5. Many justify self on other fellow's fault.
    6. "Had to go to church when a child - not now."
E. Better To Acknowledge Sins.
    1. Be willing to say "I have sinned."
    2. Some Bible examples: Saul. 1 Sam. 15:24; David; 2 Sam. 12:13; Daniel; Dan. 9:5; Achan; Josh. 7:20.

III. Conclusion.
A. Most men are guilty of self-justification. Prov. 20:6.
B. Commending self will not make us approved. 2 Cor. 10:18.
C. We should justify ourselves only by justifying God. Cf. Luke 7:29.

Departing From God
Heb. 3:12

I. Introduction.

    A. Text refers to people who are with God. Cf. Gen. 5:22; Heb. 3:1.

    B. At birth all are with God. Mt. 18:3.

    C. Being away from Him is a result of "going astray." Isa. 53:6.

    D. We are brought back by "turning to God." Acts 26:20.

    E. Sin has always been that which separates man from God. Isa. 59:2.

II. Discussion.

    A. Danger of Departing.

        1. People in kingdom will be gathered out. Jno. 3:5; Mt. 13:41-42.

        2. People may forget God and be lost. Jer. 2:32; Psa. 9:17.

        3. Better never to know truth than turn from it. 2 Pet. 2:20-21.

        4. Some shall depart from faith. 1 Tim. 4:1.

        5. May fall from grace. Gal. 5:4; 1 Cor. 10:12.

        6. God's ways are equal. Ezek. 18:21-25.

    B. Reasons For Departing.

        1. The Influence of religious leaders.

            a. Admonitions against this. Eph. 4:14; Col. 2:12.

            b. Galatians were thus influenced. Gal. 1:6-8.

            c. Israel caused to err by their leaders. Isa. 9:16.

        2. Overabundance of self-confidence.

            a. We are foolish to trust in self. Prov. 28:26.

            b. When we think we are safe we are in danger. 1 Cor. 10:12.

            c. This was Peter's fault. Lk. 22:31-33; Mark 14:27-31.

        3. The love of money.

            a. Cannot serve God and mammon. Mt. 6:24.

b. Those who covet money err from faith. 1 Tim. 6:9-10.

c. Note the case of Ananias and Sapphira. Acts 5.

4. The Effects of prosperity.

    a. God warned Israel of this danger. Deut. 8:11-14.

    b. But they forgot him. Hos. 13:6.

5. Love for the world.

    a. The force that moves forward will move backward when in reverse.

    b. Love of God and love of world don't mix. 1 Jno. 2:15.

    c. Demas an example of this. 2 Tim. 4:10. Cf. church attendance with other things.

6. Power of Persecution.

    a. This the lesson of "stony ground hearer" Mt. 13:20-21.

    b. Some were unwilling to suffer persecution. Gal. 6:12.

    c. The power of this foretold by Christ. Mt. 24:12-13.

7. Fear of Displeasing men.

    a. Pleasing man and serving Christ incompatible. Gal. 1:10.

    b. Saul failed because he "feared the people." 1 Sam. 15:24.

8. Seeking Good through Evil.

    a. Too many think the end justifies the means.

    b. Paul condemned this idea. Rom. 3:7-8.

    c. Nadab and Abihu made this mistake. Lev. 10:1-3.

9. Trying to help Lord out of difficulties.

    a. Think God's plan inadequate - legislate for Him.

    b. Uzzah got in bad on this ground. 2 Sam. 6:6-7.

10. Deceitfulness of sin.

    a. Often commit sin, thinking it not sin.

    b. Hardened by deceitfulness of sin. Heb. 3:13.

    c. Sin deceived Paul. Rom. 7:11.

C. Results Of Departing.

  1. Kept Israel out of Canaan. Heb. 3:10-11.

  2. Will keep us out of heaven. Heb. 4:1, 11.

III. Conclusion.

A. Easy to drift away from God.

B. A gradual fall is often the hardest fall.

C. Must stay with the Book to keep from falling.

God's Measuring Reed
Rev. 11:1

I. **Introduction.**
   A. Purpose of the reed to measure - various instruments used today.
   B. Importance of measuring.
      1. In mercantile affairs:
         a. To avoid cheating.
         b. To avoid being cheated.
      2. In building - that parts may properly fit.

II. **Discussion.**
   A. The Instrument Used - Word of God.
      1. Its Strength and Endurance.
         a. Symbolized by "rod." Rev. 11:1.
         b. It is quick and powerful. Heb. 4:12.
         c. It will endure forever. Isa. 40:8; Mt. 24:35.
      2. An authoritative measure.
         a. Measures authorized by Government.
         b. This one backed by God's authority. Mt. 7:28, 29.
      3. A Trustworthy measure. Psa. 119:86; Tit. 1:9.
      4. A perfect measure.
         a. Proved by its being inspired 2 Tim. 3:16-17; 2 Pet. 1:21.
         b. It is said to be perfect. Psa. 19:7; Rom. 12:2; Jas. 1:25.
      5. Not to be handled deceitfully. 2 Cor. 4:2.
         a. Some will pervert the truth. Gal. 1:6-7.
         b. It is dangerous to do so. Gal. 1:8, 9; Rev. 18, 19.
   B. Measuring The Temple (Church). Eph. 2:21-22.
      1. Its establishment. Mt. 16:18; Mk. 9:1.
      2. Its foundation.
         a. To be a tried stone. Isa. 28:16.
         b. Christ the foundation. 1 Cor. 3:10; Eph. 2:20.
      3. Its organization.
         a. Two classes of officers - elders and deacons.

Acts 20:28; 1 Tim. 3:8-13.

      b. No societies to do the work. Eph. 3:21.

    4. Its name.

      a. As a universal body. Heb. 12:23.

      b. Local congregations - churches of Christ. Rom. 16:16.

    5. Laws of admission.

      a. Faith. Heb. 11:6.

      b. Repentance Acts 17:30.

      c. Confession. Rom. 10:10.

      d. Baptism. Gal. 3:27.

C. Measuring The Altar (Worship). Heb. 13:10.

    1. Teaching apostles' doctrine. Acts 2:42.

    2. Prayer. 1 Tim. 2:8.

    3. The kind of music. Eph. 5:19; Heb. 13:15.

    4. Lord's Supper. 1 Cor. 11:23-25; Acts 20:7.

    5. Plan of raising money. 1 Cor. 16:1-2; 2 Cor. 12-14.

D. Measuring The Worshipers.

    1. As to name.

      a. Are called by many titles - saint, elect, children, etc.

      b. Christian the distinguishing name. Acts 11:26; 1 Pet. 4:14.

    2. As to Character.

      a. A holy priesthood. 1 Pet. 2:5.

      b. Obedient to God. Eccl. 12:13; Acts 10:38.

      c. Kind and loving to each other. Eph. 4:2.

    3. As to attitude in worshipping. Jno. 4:23, 24; Mt. 5:23f.

III. Conclusion.

A. The outward court (world) not measured. Rev. 11:2.

B. If not measured in you are measured out.

C. How do you compare with the measuring reed?

First Christian Grace — Virtue
2 Pet. 1:5

I. **Introduction.**
   A. No single "grace" will make a Christian.
   B. Nor can one be completely added at a time - a blending of all.
   C. Biblical number "seven" - completeness.
   D. Virtue placed in forefront - means courage.

II. **Discussion.**
   A. Courage Enjoined.
   1. In Old Testament.
      a. Upon Joshua who succeeded Moses. Josh. 1:6-9.
      b. Upon Israel in general. Josh. 23:1-6.
   2. In New Testament.
      a. Upon disciples by Christ. Mt. 10:28.
      b. Also enjoined by Paul. 1 Cor. 16:13; Phil. 1:27, 28.
   B. When Courage Is Needed.
   1. When In The Minority.
      a. Promise to two or three. Mt. 18:20.
      b. Majority usually in the wrong. Mt. 7:13-14.
      c. Strength not always with the majority. Lev. 26:8.
      d. Examples of courage when in minority.
         (1) Joshua and Caleb against ten spies. Num. 13:26-33; 14:6-10.
         (2) Gideon's army of 300 men. Judg. 7:1-12.
         (3) Paul once stood alone. 2 Tim. 4:16-17.
   2. When civil laws conflict with God's laws.
      a. Obey civil laws when no conflict. Rom. 13:1.
      b. Examples of courage of this kind.
         (1) Three Hebrews respecting Nebuchadnezzar's image. Dan. 3:16-18.
         (2) Daniel respecting the king's decree. Dan. 6:10.
         (3) Apostles at different times. Acts 4:19-20;

5:29.
3. Under severe temptation.
   a. Temptation endured is for our good. Jas. 1:12.
   b. May have manifold temptations. 1 Pet. 1:6 (elaborate) have courage to say, "no."
   c. Joseph an example. Gen. 39:7-9.
4. When reproving those who sin.
   a. Easy to tell the other fellow about some one's sin.
   b. But admonished to rebuke those who sin. Lk. 17:3; 1 Tim. 5:20; Tit. 1:13.
   c. Examples of courage of this kind.
      (1) Nathan in rebuking David. 2 Sam. 12:1-7.
      (2) Peter in rebuking Ananias & wife (Acts 5:1-5) and Simon (Acts 8:20-23).
      (3) Paul in withstanding Peter. Gal. 2:11-13.
5. When Obedience to God seems unreasonable.
   a. He requires but a reasonable service. Rom. 12:1; 1 Jno. 5:3.
   b. Abraham a worthy example. Gen. 12:1-4; 22:1-14.
6. When Preaching truth under persecution.
   a. Easy to preach when there is no danger.
   b. But danger must not turn us back.
   c. Examples of courage of this kind.
      (1) Stephen before the Jews. Acts 7.
      (2) Paul could not be moved. Acts 20:22-24; 21:13.

C. Results of Courage.
   1. May get us into trouble here.
   2. But will prove our sincerity to others. Acts 4:13.
   3. Will mean much to us hereafter. Rev. 2:10.

III. Conclusion.

A. Proper faith in God will give us courage. Prov. 14:26; Eph. 3:12.
B. Can do all things through Christ who strengthens. Phil. 4:13.

Weighed In The Balances
Dan. 5:27

I. Introduction.

    A. Relate story of Belshazzar's feast. Dan. 5:1-5.

    B. Describe the effect on the revelers. Dan. 5:6.

    C. Note the failure of the magicians. Dan. 5:7-9.

    D. Give Daniel's interpretation of handwriting. Dan. 5:10-28.

    E. People concerned about body - Lord weighs soul. Prov. 16:2; 1 Sam. 2:3.

    F. Imagine balance on stand - each to be weighed.

II. Discussion.

    A. Various Characters Weighed.

        1. The Idolater.

            a. The weight: "Shalt have no other gods." Ex. 20:3; Acts 14:15; 1 Jno. 5:21.

            b. Not worship likenessess. Crosses, crucifixes, pictures of Christ, etc.

            c. Tekel: "No inheritance in kingdom." Eph. 5:5.

        2. The Drunkard.

            a. The weight: "Be not drunk" Eph. 5:18; Rom. 13:13.

            b. Tekel: "Not inherit the kingdom." 1 Cor. 6:10.

        3. The Murderer.

            a. The weight: "Shall not kill." Rom. 13:9; 1 Pet. 5:15.

            b. May be a murderer at heart. 1 Jno. 3:15.

            c. Tekel: "No eternal life." 1 Jno. 3:15.

        4. The Liar.

            a. The weight: "Not bear false witness." Rom. 13:9; Col. 3:9.

            b. Deception of any kind is a lie.

            c. Tekel: "Have part in lake of fire." Rev. 21:8.

        5. The Thief.

            a. The weight: "Shalt not steal." Rom. 13:9; Eph.

4:28.

      b. Tekel: "Not inherit the kingdom." 1 Cor. 6:10.

6. The Adulterer.

      a. The weight: "Shalt not commit adultery." Rom. 13:9.

      b. Adultery may be in act or thought. Jno. 8:3; Mt. 5:28.

      c. Tekel: "Not inherit the kingdom." 1 Cor. 6:9.

7. The Blasphemer.

      a. The weight: "Not take God's name in vain." Ex. 20:7; 2 Tim. 3:2.

      b. People come dangerously near. "Great am I," "Good Lord," etc.

      c. Tekel: "Not hold him guiltless." Ex. 20:7.

8. The unbeliever.

      a. The weight: "Must believe." Heb. 11:6.

      b. Tekel: "Die in sins." Jno. 8:24.

9. The Impenitent.

      a. The weight: "Commanded all to repent." Acts 17:20.

      b. Heaven will rejoice over one who repents. Lk. 15:7.

      c. Tekel: "Shall perish." Luke 13:3; Rom. 2:5.

10. The non-confessor.

      a. The weight: "Shalt confess." Rom. 10:9-10.

      b. Tekel: "Will be denied." Mt. 10:32, 33.

11. The unbaptized.

      a. The weight: "Be baptized for remission." Acts 2:38; Mk. 16:16.

      b. To fail is to reject counsel of God. Lk. 7:29, 30.

      c. Tekel: "Vengeance on them that obey not." 2 Thess. 1:8.

12. The moralist.

      a. The weight: "Must be born again." Jno. 3:7; Mt. 18:3.

      b. Tekel: "No escape to disobedient." Heb. 2:2, 3.

13. The backslider.

      a. The weight: "Hold fast without wavering." Heb. 10:2, 3.

      b. Tekel: "Latter end worse than beginning." 2 Pet. 2:21, 22.

III. Conclusion.

A. All will be weighed at the judgment.

B. If we weigh ourselves as we go along we can supply what is "wanting."

C. Must not weigh in our own balances.

Second Christian Grace — Knowledge
2 Pet. 1:5

I. **Introduction.**
   A. Courage without knowledge of little benefit. Cf. Rom. 10:1-3.
   B. Pursue knowledge from childhood to old age. "Never too old to learn."
   C. Not surprising that it is given as a Christian characteristic.
   D. Might be worldly wise and destitute of this. Cf. 1 Tim. 2:4; 6:20.

II. **Discussion.**
   A. Knowledge Enjoined.
      1. By the apostle Peter. 2 Pet. 1:5; 3:18.
      2. By the apostle Paul. Rom. 16:19; 1 Cor. 14:20.
   B. Things We Need To Know.
      1. The will of God. Eph. 5:17.
         a. Can't even become Christian otherwise. 1 Tim. 2:4; Heb. 8:10, 11: Mt. 13:10, 23; Rom. 6:17-18.
         b. Can't live Christian without it. Col. 1:9-10.
      2. The love of Christ. Eph. 3:17-19.
         a. The breadth of his love. Jno. 3:16; Mk. 16:15.
         b. The length of his love. 1 Cor. 13:8.
         c. The depth of his love. 1 Tim. 1:15.
         d. The height of his love. Jno. 14:1-3.
      3. The hope of God's calling. Eph. 1:18.
         a. It is a blessed hope. Tit. 2:13.
         b. An anchor of the soul. Heb. 6:19. "set before us."
         c. One hope of our calling. Eph. 4:4.
      4. The riches of his glory. Eph. 1:18.
         a. God purposed to make known these riches. Rom. 9:23.
         b. They shall supply our every need. Phil. 4:19.
         c. Christ became poor that we might be rich. 2 Cor.

8:9.

5. The greatness of His power. Eph. 1:19.
   a. Was longsuffering to make it known. Rom. 9:22.
   b. It raised and exalted Christ. Eph. 1:20-22.
   c. Will likewise raise us. 1 Cor. 6:14.

C. Why We Need To Know These.
   1. Ignorance of His will won't excuse.
      a. Ignorance alienates from God. Eph. 4:18.
      b. All commanded to repent. Acts 17:30.
      c. Paul prayed that ignorant folks might be saved. Rom. 10:1-3.
   2. Love of Christ begets love. 1 Jno. 4:19.
   3. Hope influences us.
      a. Temples sorrows of earth. 1 Cor. 15:19; 1 Thess. 4:13.
      b. By it we are saved. Rom. 8:24; leads us to joys of heaven.
   4. Riches create desire. Luke 16:11; 1 Tim. 6:17.
   5. His power keeps us. 1 Pet. 1:5.
      a. Given all we need. 2 Pet. 1:3.
      b. Knowledge of his power increases our faith.

D. The Source of Knowledge.
   1. Treasures of wisdom and knowledge in Christ. Col. 2:3.
   2. Obtained by study. Psa. 119:104; 2 Tim. 2:15; 3:15; Eph. 3:4.
   3. Apply to "things we need to know."

E. Results of Knowledge.
   1. It may puff us up. 1 Cor. 8:1, 2.
   2. Should cause us to grow. 2 Pet. 3:18.
   3. Increases our responsibility. Lk. 12:47; Jas. 4:17.

III. **Conclusion.**
   A. Often responsible for our ignorance. Rom. 1:28; Mt. 13:15.
   B. Eternal measures rest there with us.
   C. Should realize how little we know - strive to know more.

The Greatest Insurance Company
Jno. 3:36

I. **Introduction.**
   A. This an age of insurance - fire, sickness, accident, death.
   B. None of those insure the soul for eternity.
   C. Material interests are insignificant compared to eternal. Mt. 16:26.
   D. Must use accomodated terms - Bible nowhere calls it this.

II. **Discussion.**
   A. The Company Described.
      1. The church is the company.
         a. Established in AD 33. Mk. 9:1; Acts 2:1-4.
         b. The name of the company. Heb. 12:23; Rom. 16:16; 1 Cor. 1:2.
         c. Salvation placed in it. 2 Tim. 2:10.
      2. Christ is the Head. Eph. 1:22, 23; Col. 1:18.
         a. Members must be subject to him. Eph. 5:24.
      3. The agents.
         a. The apostles the first sent out. Mt. 28:19, 20; Mk. 16:15, 16.
         b. Then "faithful men" selected. 2 Tim. 2:2.
         c. Reward for their service. Dan. 12:3; 1 Cor. 3:12-14.
   B. Financial Conditions of Company.
      1. The assets of the company.
         a. Assets defined: "Property subject to payments of debts."
         b. Cash capital - "unsearchable riches." Eph. 3:8.
         c. Surplus - "More than needed." Eph. 3:20.
      2. The liabilities of the company.
         a. Liabilities defined: "Debts of obligations."
         b. Liabilities of policies "all our needs." Phil. 4:19; 2 Cor. 9:8.

        c. Net policy reserves - "for all who will" Heb. 7:25.
   C. Policy Described.
        1. The only policy that insures for eternity.
             a. Insures against eternal death. Rom. 6:23; Rev.
                 2:11.
             b. Insures against eternal fire. Mt. 25:41; Rev.
                 20:15.
             c. Insures for eternal life. Mt. 25:46; 1 Jno. 2:25.
        2. Present health conditions not considered. Isa. 1:18;
             1 Tim. 1:15; Rev. 22:17.
        3. Age limit - maturity to death.
        4. Dividends begin from date of policy. Eph. 1:3; Mk.
             10:28-30.
        5. Conditions of the policy.
             a. Faith. Jno. 3:36.
             b. Repentance. Acts 11:18.
             c. Confession. Rom. 10:9-10.
             d. Baptism. Rom. 6:3-4.
        6. The policy may be forfeited.
             a. Must be faithful till death. Rev. 2:10; Mt. 24:12,
                 13.
             b. May become a castaway. 1 Cor. 9:27; 2 Pet. 2:20,
                 21.
   D. Beneficiaries.
        1. Husband's policy can't be made to wife nor wife's to
             husband (elaborate).
        2. Every person his own beneficiary. Rom. 14:12; 1
             Cor. 3:8.
   E. Neglecting To Sign.
        1. Many people plan to insure for time but neglect.
        2. More neglect to insure for eternity. Cf. Heb. 2:3.

III. **Conclusion.**
   A. Insurance agent asks: "What becomes of family if you
        die?"
   B. More important: What will become of you?

Third Christian Grace — Temperance
2 Pet. 1:6

I. Introduction.

  A. Temperance defined: "Self-control."

  B. This an indispensable part of a Christian character.

  C. All do not need it with respect to same thing temperaments differ.

  D. But none have reached the place where it is not needed.

II. Discussion.

  A. Temperance Enjoined.

    1. In the text by Peter.

    2. Likewise enjoined by Paul.

      a. On bishops of congregations. Tit. 1:8.

      b. On aged men and women. Tit. 2:2, 3.

      c. All should live "soberly." Tit. 2:12.

  B. Wherein Temperance Is Needed.

    1. With respect to strong drink.

      a. This the usual understanding of temperance.

      b. Drunkenness forbidden. Prov. 20:1; Rom. 13:13; Eph. 5:18; 1 Thess. 5:7, 8.

      c. Daniel totally abstained from king's drink. Dan. 1:8, 12.

    2. With respect to opinions.

      a. All people have opinions - Ill. by Nicodemus coming to Jesus by night.

      b. But must control them - not force them on others. Rom. 14:22.

    3. With respect to language.

      a. Often cultivate "by-words" that are worse than useless.

      b. Commanded to bridle the tongue. Jas. 3:3-10; 1:26.

      c. If filthy jokes tempt, we must refrain. Eph. 4:29; 5:4.

      d. David an example of controlling tongue. Psa. 39:1.

4. With respect to tattling.
    a. It is so easy to talk about someone. Cf. 1 Tim. 5:13.
    b. Self-control is required. 2 Thess. 3:11; 1 Pet. 4:15.

5. With respect to pride.
    a. "A little learning is a dangerous thing." Cf. 1 Cor. 8:1.
    b. Easy to become self-infatuated. Gal. 6:3.
    c. A little honor may be our ruin. 1 Tim. 3:6.
    d. Must humble ourselves. Jas. 4:10; 1 Pet. 5:6.
    e. Daniel an example of self-control in this. Dan. 2:30.

6. With respect to covetousness.
    a. We are usually dissatisfied with our own state.
    b. Covetousness strictly forbidden. Rom. 13:9; Eph. 5:3.
    c. Desire for wealth often leads to ruin. 1 Tim. 6:9f.
    d. Paul an example of self-control. Acts 20:33.

7. With respect to fleshly desires.
    a. All human beings have passions of various kinds.
    b. But they must be restrained. Rom. 13:14; 1 Pet. 2:11; 1 John 2:16.
    c. Some examples of self-control.
       (1) Joseph in Potipher's house. Gen. 39:7-9.
       (2) Paul kept body in subjection. 1 Cor. 9:27.

8. With respect to Anger.
    a. "No one loses his temper unless he has too much."
    b. The more we lose our temper, the more we have.
    c. Naaman almost made fatal mistake here. 2 Kg. 5:12.
    d. Anger must be restrained. Prov. 16:32; 19:11; Mt. 5:22; Eph. 4:26; Jas. 1:19-20.

9. With respect to Revenge.
    a. Uncontrolled anger leads to revenge.
    b. But revenge is forbidden. Prov. 24:29; Rom. 12:17-19; 1 Thess. 5:15.

10. With respect to all things. 1 Cor. 9:25.

III. Conclusion.
A. Temperance a fruit of spirit. Gal. 5:23 - must be cultivated.
B. Felix trembled over this proposition. Acts 24:25.
C. It will mean much to us at the judgment.

The Witness Of The Spirit
Rom. 8:16

I. **Introduction.**
   A. Before testimony can be given, the fact must exist.
      1. Geo. Washington became president before testimoney of it.
      2. Must be children of God before Spirit witnesses to it.
   B. Faith is based on testimony.
   C. Testimony must be suited to hearers. Ill. by interpreter.

II. **Discussion.**
   A. A Witness Defined.
      1. One that tells something he knows.
         a. Things known by five senses, but no one thing by all.
         b. Jesus said, "We testify that we have seen." Jno. 3:11; Cf. 3:12.
         c. Apostles witnesses "because had been with him. Jno. 15:27.
         d. Had to be "witnesses of resurrection." Acts 1:21, 22.
         e. Were "eyewitnesses of his majesty." 2 Pet. 1:16.
   B. Two Witnesses Required.
      1. This a requirement of Old Testament. Deut. 17:6; Heb. 10:28.
      2. Also of the New. Matt. 18:16; 2 Cor. 13:1; 1 Tim. 5:19.
      3. Text presents two - Holy Spirit and our spirit.
   C. How Testimony Is Born.
      1. Men bear witness by means of words. 1 Kings 21:10; Mt. 18:16; 26:60-62.
      2. God bore witness the same way. Heb. 1:1, 2.
         a. When he bore witness to Abel. Heb. 11:4.
         b. And when He witnessed of Christ. Jno. 5:37; Mt. 3:17; 1 Jno. 5:8-10.

152

3. John the baptist did likewise. Jno. 1:7; 32-34; 3:25f.
4. Old Testament bears witness in words. Jno. 5:39.
5. Apostles thus gave their testimony. Mt. 10:18-19.
   a. People to believe "through their word." Jno. 17:26.
   b. Commanded to testify thus. Acts 10:39-42.
D. Testimony of Holy Spirit.
   1. The Spirit "speaketh expressly." 1 Tim. 4:1; Cf. Jno. 16:13; Acts 20:23.
   2. He spoke through the prophets.
      a. In Old Testament dispensations. 2 Sam. 23:2; Neh. 9:30; 1 Pet. 1:10; 2 Pet. 1:21.
      b. A New Testament example. Acts 11:27, 28.
   3. He spoke through the apostles. Jno. 14:26; Acts 2:1-11; 1 Pet. 1:12; Mt. 10:19, 20.
   4. He speaks through the gospel. 1 Cor. 2:4; 1 Thess. 1:5.
E. Agreement Of Witnesses.
   1. Bears witness "with," not "to" our spirit.
   2. Spirit says "believe." Acts 16:31 - Our spirit accepts.
   3. Spirit says "repent." Acts 17:30 - Our spirit accepts.
   4. Spirit says "confess." Rom. 10:9, 10 - Our spirit accepts.
   5. Spirit says "be baptized." Acts 2:38 - Our spirit accepts.
   6. Spirit says those who do these are "children of God." Gal. 3:26; 2 Cor. 6:17, 18; 1 Jno. 4:14; Gal. 3:27. Our spirit says we have done them.
F. Disagreeing With The Testimony.
   1. To say we can be saved without conditions. Heb. 5:8, 9.
   2. To say we can be saved by faith alone. Jas. 2:24.
   3. To say confession is unnecessary. Rom. 14:11.
   4. To say baptism is a non-essential. 1 Pet. 3:21.

III. **Conclusion.**
A. To disagree is to resist the Spirit.
B. People were condemned for this. Acts 7:51.
C. Condemned for resisting truth. 2 Tim. 3:8; Lk. 7:29-30.

Fourth Christian Grace — Patience
2 Pet. 1:6

I. **Introduction.**

    A. A very precious Christian grace, but difficult to add.

    B. We need it in the zeal and eagerness of youth.

    C. Needed in firm purpose and severe tempers of manhood.

    D. Also in despondencies and gloom of old age.

    E. Patience defined - "Uncomplaining endurance."

II. **Discussion.**

    A. Patience Enjoined.

        1. Peter says in text to add it.

        2. Paul enjoined it upon servants of God. 1 Tim. 6:11; 2 Tim. 2:24.

        3. Upon the brethren by James. Jas. 5:7.

    B. Wherein Patience Is Needed.

        1. In tribulation. Rom. 12:12.

            a. No glory to suffer for own faults. 1 Pet. 2:20.

            b. Thankworthy to suffer for Christ. Mt. 5:11, 12; 1 Pet. 2:19, 20; 4:12, 13.

            c. Some examples of patience in tribulation.

                (1) Christ the greatest example. 1 Pet. 2:21-23.

                (2) The Thessalonians. 1 Thess. 2:14; 2 Thess. 1:4.

                (3) The prophets cited by James, Jas. 5:10; Cf. Acts 7:52; 2 Chron. 36:15-16.

        2. In well doing. Rom. 2:7.

            a. Must commit souls to God in well doing. 1 Pet. 4:19.

            b. Must not become weary. Gal. 6:9; 2 Thess. 3:13.

            c. Service to God not in vain. 1 Cor. 15:58; 1 Pet. 2:15.

        3. In dealing with disorderly.

            a. With patience warn unruly. 1 Thess. 5:14.

            b. Restore in meekness, considering self. Gal. 6:1.

  c. Admonish as a brother. 2 Thess. 3:15.
  4. In Christian race. Heb. 12:1.
    a. Hardships and difficulties to meet.
    b. Continuous race. Must run to end. Mt. 24:12, 13.
  5. In Vexations of life.
    a. May be properly vexed at sin. 2 Pet. 2:7, 8.
    b. Little vexations must not upset us - flat tires, etc.
     Cf. Jas. 1:19-20; Eph. 4:26.
    c. The fool rageth and is confident. Prov. 14:16.
  6. With regard to each other.
    a. Should be peacemakers. Mt. 5:9; Prov. 15:18.
    b. Forbearing one another in love. Eph. 4:2.
  7. In waiting for reward. Rom. 8:25.
    a. Farmer given as illustration. Jas. 5:7, 8.
    b. Don't decide Lord delays coming. 2 Pet. 3:3; 4;
     Lk. 12:45, 46.
C. The Cause of Patience.
  1. Tribulation worketh patience. Rom. 5:3; Jas. 1:3.
  2. Examples of others move us to patience. Heb. 6:12.
    a. Apply to examples of Christ, prophets and Job
     previously mentioned.
D. Results of Patience.
  1. Helps us to be an influence for good here.
  2. Prepares for eternal reward hereafter. Lk. 21:19;
    Rom. 15:4; Heb. 10:36.

III. Conclusion.

A. Patient in spirit is better than proud. Eccl. 7:8, 9.

B. Not always best to say what you think.

C. Patience doesn't conflict with courage.

Fifth Christian Grace — Godliness
2 Pet. 1:6

I. **Introduction.**
   A. Godliness means God-likeness - God revealed in us.
   B. There is no greater characteristic of Christianity.
   C. Eliminate godliness and Christianity ceases.
   D. Labor and time spent without it are wasted.

II. **Discussion.**
   A. Godliness Enjoined.
      1. By Peter. 2 Pet. 1:6; 3:11.
      2. By Paul.
         a. Exercise thyself unto godliness. 1 Tim. 4:7.
         b. Deny ungodliness and live godly. Tit. 2:11-13; 1 Tim. 6:10, 11.
         c. Serve God with reverence and godly fear. Heb. 12:28.
   B. How We May Be Like God.
      1. In Love.
         a. Even loved us while we were sinners. Jno. 3:16; Rom. 5:8; Eph. 2:4, 5.
         b. We must love him in return. Mt. 22:37; 1 Jno. 4:19.
         c. Must love the brethren. 1 Jno. 3:10; 4:7, 11.
         d. Also love the unrighteous. Mt. 5:43-47.
      2. In Impartiality.
         a. He is no respecter of persons. 2 Chron. 19:7; Acts 10:34, 35; 1 Pet. 1:17.
         b. This is required of us. Jas. 2:1-4, 9.
      3. In longsuffering.
         a. Always been longsuffering with man. 1 Pet. 3:20; 2 Pet. 3:9, 15.
         b. Men have taken advantage of it. Eccl. 8:11; Rom. 2:4, 5.
         c. We must be longsuffering. Eph. 4:2; Col. 1:11.
      4. In mercy.

        a. Mercy is an attribute of God. Dan. 9:9; Eph. 2:4; Tit. 3:5.

        b. We should be like him. Lk. 6:36; Mt. 5:7; Jas. 2:13.

    5. In Justice.

        a. Justice is habitation of God's throne. Psa. 89:14; Cf. Job 37:23.

        b. We should be just in our dealings. Gen. 18:19; Psa. 82:23f; Tit. 1:8.

    6. In Holiness.

        a. He is holy in all his works. Psa. 145:17.

        b. Must imitate him. Mt. 5:48; 1 Pet. 1:15-16. Cf. 1 Sam. 2:2.

        c. Be holy in words. Eph. 4:29; and deeds. 1 Pet. 1:15; 2 Pet. 3:11.

    7. By standing for the truth.

        a. Truth of Lord endures forever. Psa. 117:2.

        b. Revealed all things that pertain to godliness. 2 Pet. 1:3.

          (1) No need to go elsewhere to learn religious service.

        c. Must teach truth which is according to godliness. 1 Tim. 6:3; Tit. 1:1.

C. Godliness Misconstrued.

    1. Some suppose that gain is godliness. 1 Tim. 6:5; Cf. Tit. 1:11.

    2. Outward form of godliness. 2 Tim. 3:5; Cf. Mt. 23:14, 27, 28.

D. Results of Godliness.

    1. It insures persecution. 2 Tim. 3:12; Lk. 6:26.

    2. Works deliverance from temptation. 2 Pet. 2:9; 1 Cor. 10:13.

    3. With contentment is great gain. 1 Tim. 6:6; Rom. 8:31; Mt. 6:33.

    4. Prepares us for life to come. 1 Tim. 4:8.

III. Conclusion.

A. Should pray for conditions favorable to godliness. 1 Tim. 2:2.

B. Godly is set apart for the Lord. Psa. 4:3.

C. Good works become professors of godliness. 1 Tim. 2:10.

D. If like him here, we'll be like him hereafter. Psa. 17:15; 1 Jno. 3:2.

A New Way
Heb. 10:19, 20

I. **Introduction.**
  A. Comment on text.
  B. Usually seek to know new things. Cf. Acts 17:21.
  C. New ways in religion are continually being sought.
  D. Not a new patch on old garment. Mt. 9:16, 17.
  E. This new way is old and new.
   1. Old in point of time - in existence near 2,000 yrs.
   2. New in contrast to old system; new to many who have not learned it, etc.

II. **Discussion.**
  A. A New Covenant. Jer. 31:31-34; Heb. 8:8-13.
   1. Old on stone. Ex. 32:15 - New in the heart. 2 Cor. 3:3.
   2. Old was faulty. Heb. 8:7. New is perfect. Heb. 7:19; Jas. 1:25.
   3. Old, a system of bondage. Acts 15:10 - New, a system of liberty. Gal. 5:1-2.
   4. Old to Jews. Eph. 2:12 - New to all nations. Eph. 2:13-14.
   5. Old had infant membership - New does not. Jer. 31:34.
   6. Old taken away - New established. Heb. 10:9.
  B. A New Passover.
   1. A lamb required under old system. Ex. 12:5; 21, 27
   2. Christ is our passover. 1 Cor. 5:7; 1 Pet. 1:19.
  C. A New Birth.
   1. Children of Abraham by fleshly birth. Gen. 17:13.
   2. Children new by spiritual birth. Jno. 3:3-5; 1 Pet. 2:23.
     a. New birth makes new creatures. 1 Pet. 2:2.
     b. Made new creatures "in Christ" Gal. 6:15; 2 Cor. 5:17.
     c. How get "into Christ?"

           (1) **Believe unto.** Rom. 10:10.

           (2) **Repent unto.** Acts 11:18.

           (3) **Confess unto.** Rom. 10:10.

           (4) **Baptized into.** Gal. 3:26-27. Note various results of being in Christ.

        d. May then walk in newness of life. Rom. 6:3, 4.

D. A New Name.

    1. Israel name of God's people under law. 2 Kg. 17:34; Deut. 28:10.

    2. But prophet spoke of a new name. Isa. 62:2, 3.

        a. This new name is Christian. Acts 11:26.

        b. Endorsed by the apostles. Acts 26:28, 29; 1 Pet. 4:16.

E. A New System of Worship.

    1. A new day observed.

        a. Sabbath in memory of Israel's deliverance. (Deut. 5:15) abolished Col. 2:14-17.

        b. The Lord's day in memory of Christ. Rev. 1:10; 1 Cor. 16:1, 2; Acts 20:7.

    2. A new supper observed. Matt. 26:26-28.

    3. New sacrifices offered. Heb. 9:8-10; 1 Pet. 2:5; Rom. 12:1.

    4. New praise offering given. Lev. 7:12; Heb. 13:15.

        a. This is accomplished by prayer. Phil. 4:6.

        b. Also by making melody in heart. Eph. 5:19; Col. 3:16.

F. New Promises.

    1. Founded upon better promises. Heb. 7:19; 8:6; 11:39, 40; 12:24.

    2. Some of the promises.

        a. Remission of sins. Heb. 8:12; 10:4.

        b. Eternal life beyond. 1 Jno. 2:25.

III. Conclusion.

A. This new way is a living way - text.

B. It was inaugurated by a life-giving spirit. Cf. 1 Cor. 15:45.

C. None can afford to miss it. Mt. 7:13-14.

Sixth Christian Grace —
Brotherly Kindness
2 Pet. 1:7

I. **Introduction.**
   A. Brotherly kindness closely attend to brotherly love.
   B. May be translated, "love of the brethren."
   C. Might consider love the cause and kindness the effect.
   D. Some statements on brotherly love. Jno. 13:34, 35; 1 Pet. 1:22; 1 Jno. 4:21.

II. **Discussion.**
   A. Brotherly Kindness Enjoined.
      1. In the Old Testament. Zech. 7:8-10; Deut. 22:1.
      2. In the New Testament.
         a. By Peter. 2 Pet. 1:7; 1 Pet. 2:17.
         b. By Paul. Eph. 4:32; Col. 3:12.
   B. How Brotherly Kindness May Be Shown?
      1. Through our Conversation.
         a. Should speak kindly to each other.
            (1) Law of kindness may be in tongue. Prov. 31:26.
            (2) Tremendous possibilities found in the tongue. Prov. 18:21; 15:20; 15:4.
            (3) Soft answer turneth away wrath. Prov. 15:1; Cf. Col. 4:6; Eph. 4:31, 32.
            (4) Must not call brother "Raca." Matt. 5:22.
      2. Through Sympathy.
         a. Rejoice or suffer with each other. Rom. 12:13; 1 Cor. 12:25, 26; Heb. 13:3.
         b. Onesiphorus was kind to Paul. 2 Tim. 1:16-18.
         c. Christ demonstrated this compassionate characteristic. Mt. 14:14.
      3. By Assisting The Needy.
         a. Commanded to bear each other's burdens. Gal. 6:2; Rom. 15:1-2; Phil. 2:4.
         b. Christ taught the value of giving. Mt. 5:42; Acts

20:35.

        c. If brother in need, turn him not away. Jas. 2:15; 1 Jno. 3:17.

   4. By Restoring Those Who Sin.

        a. Our friends are those who tell us of our faults. Cf. Mt. 18:15.

        b. To show interest in restoring one is kindness. Jas. 5:19-20.

        c. Must be done in spirit of meekness. Gal. 6:1.

   5. By Forgiveness.

        a. Relate parable of unmerciful debtor. Mt. 18:23f.

        b. Must forgive even as God forgave. Eph. 4:32; Col. 3:12.

        c. Must forgive as often as asked. Lk. 17:3-4; Mt. 18:21, 22.

   6. By Practicing Golden Rule.

        a. The golden rule given by Christ. Mt. 7:12.

        b. Not a negative but a positive rule - must do something.

        c. Not be as kind to others as they are to you.

        d. To ascertain its meaning, change places with the other fellow.

   7. By Doing Good For Evil.

        a. Anyone can return good for good. Mt. 5:46.

        b. But we are to return good for evil. 1 Pet. 3:8-9.

        c. Evil can't overcome evil, no more than fire can put out fire. Cf. Rom. 12:17-21.

        d. Two wrongs will not make one right.

   8. By Respecting Conscience of Others.

        a. Must not make stumbling block of our liberty. 1 Cor. 8:9; Rom. 14:13.

        b. Sacrifice our rights to avoid offending. Rom. 14:21; 1 Cor. 8:13.

        c. Gospel must not be sacrifice for any one's conscience.

   9. By Preferring Each Other.

        a. In honor preferring one another. Rom. 12:15.

        b. Do good to all - especially household of faith. Gal. 6:10.

III. Conclusion.

A. To oppress the poor is to reproach God. Prov. 14:31.

B. When we sin against brethren we sin against Christ. 1 Cor. 8:12; Acts 9:4.

C. Our actions toward brethren will meet us at the judgment. Matt. 25:31-46; Heb. 6:10.

The Evidence Of Pardon
Heb. 11:1

I. **Introduction.**
   A. Pardon is very important to every soul.
   B. The best of evidence should be desired.
   C. Three theories - cannot know; know by feelings; know by faith.

II. **Discussion.**
   A. The Value of Evidence.
   1. Valuable in affairs of life - court trials, science, evolution.
   2. Evidence of Divinity of Bible important.
       a. No contradictions found in it.
       b. Man has never written one the equal of it.
       c. Fulfilled prophecy an unmistakable proof.
   3. Evidence of resurrection of Christ of great value. Acts 1:3.
   4. Evidence of pardon likewise valuable, "am I his or am I not?"
   B. Is Knowledge Possible? (Relative)
   1. "I know that my redeemer liveth." Job 19:25.
   2. Know assuredly Jesus is Lord. Acts 2:36.
   3. Know all things work for good. Rom. 8:28.,
   4. Know we have a building of God. 2 Cor. 5:1.
   5. Know we'll be like him. 1 Jno. 3:2.
   6. In same sense may know we are pardoned. 1 Jno. 2:3; 3:14.
   C. Pardon Explained.
   1. Not a change of heart - that takes place in man.
   2. It is remission or forgiveness. Jer. 31:34: 33:8; 50:20.
   3. It takes place in heaven.
       a. God does the pardoning. Isa. 55:7; 1 Kg. 8:44, 45.
       b. Occurs in the mind of God. Heb. 8:12.

      c. Illustrate by pardon issued by Governor.

D. Feelings Are Unreliable.
1. Feelings are evidence of physical facts.
    a. May determine if things are hot, cold, hard, soft, painful, etc.
    b. But false conclusions may be drawn even in this. Gen. 27:1-29.
    c. Sin is not a physical, material substance. 1 Jno. 3:4; 5:17.
      (1) Neither the sin nor the forgiveness of it can be felt.
2. Christians have no confidence in the flesh. Phil. 3.
3. If feelings the evidence - religion on level with the beast. Jude 10.
4. Emotional nature cannot be depended on.
    a. Imaginative pot of gold; wrong highway; false report of friend's death.
    b. Some examples of deceptive emotions.
      (1) Jacob at report of Joseph's death. Gen. 37.
      (2) Naaman thought prophet would come out. 2 Kg. 5:11.
      (3) Heathen think they'll be heard for much speaking. Mt. 6:7.
      (4) Saul of Tarsus. Acts 23:1; 24:16; 26:9. Cf. Jno. 16:2.
      (5) Religion of the Hindu mother.
5. How know we have right feelings if never experienced before?
6. To trust in own heart is foolish. Prov. 28:26; Jer. 17:9.
7. Can't tell by feelings what is in God's mind. (Governor illustration.)

E. The Proper Evidence.
1. We walk by faith. 2 Cor. 5:7; Heb. 11:1.
    a. To walk by feelings evidence of blindness.
    b. Not how faith comes. Rom. 10:17; Acts 15:7.
2. Word of God the infallible proof. Heb. 2:1-3; Jno. 20:30, 31; 1 Jno. 3:14; 5:13.
3. Some want more evidence - doubt God's word. Cf. Luke 16:27-31.
4. We know him if we keep his commandments. 1 Jno. 2:3.
    a. Apply to commandments necessary to salvation. Faith, Repentance, confession and baptism.

III. Conclusion.

A. Religion has always been system of faith and practice. Cf. Jas. 1:27.

B. If we do what God says, no need to fear results.

Seventh Christian Grace — Charity
2 Pet. 1:7

I. **Introduction.**
   A. Think of charity as outward acts, but it is the prompting principle.
   B. God's love prompted the gift of Christ, the gift was the act of love. Jno. 3:16; Rom. 5:8; 1 Jno. 4:9.
   C. Charitable acts might exist without love, but love can't exist long without acts.

II. **Discussion.**
   A. Importance of Christian Charity.
      1. Without it, may speak all tongues - be as sounding brass. 1 Cor. 13:1.
      2. Gift of prophecy - knowledge of future - yet be nothing. 1 Cor. 13:2.
      3. Understand all mysteries and knowledge (elaborate) yet be nothing. 1 Cor. 13:2.
      4. Have all faith - miraculous - yet be nothing. 1 Cor. 13:2.
      5. Making sacrifices without it - no profit. 1 Cor. 13:3.
         a. "Bestow all my goods to feed the poor."
            (1) This seems impossible but it is not.
            (2) Outward liberality may arise from motives of pure display. Mt. 6:1, 2.
            (3) It may arise from rigid sense of duty - not prompted by love.
         b. May give our bodies to be burned - suffer death.
      6. Importance shown by promises based on it.
         a. God dwells in us. 1 Jno. 4:16.
         b. Many things prepared. 1 Cor. 2:9.
         c. Will be heirs of kingdom. Jas. 2:5.
         d. Will receive a crown of life. Jas. 1:12.
   B. Characteristics of Christian Charity.
      1. Patience - "Suffereth long." 1 Cor. 13:4.
         a. Patience is enduring love - when it ceases to be

166

patient, it ceases to be love.

    b. When persecuted, suffer without complaining. 1 Pet. 2:19-21.

    c. In patience possess your souls. Lk. 21:19; Heb. 10:36.

2. Kindness "is kind." 1 Cor. 13:4.

    a. Kindness is love at work, love in action. Cf. Eph. 4:32.

    b. To be kind to God, must be kind to his children. 1 Cor. 8:12; Acts 9:4; Matt. 25:31-46.

3. Liberality - "Envieth not" 1 Cor. 13:4.

    a. Not made unhappy by the good fortunes of others. Cf. Gen. 4:4-8; Acts 7:9; Dan. 6:4; Mark 15:10.

    b. Charity rejoices at happiness of others. Rom. 12:15; 1 Cor. 12:26.

4. Humility - "Vaunteth not itself, not puffed up." 1 Cor. 13:4.

    a. Makes no display of itself - sounds no trumpet. Mt. 6:2.

    b. Pride will ruin a person. Prov. 16:18; 18:12; 29:23; 1 Tim. 3:6.

    c. Humility is the way to real greatness. Mt. 18:1-4; 1 Pet. 5:6; Phil. 2:3.

5. Courtesy - "Doth not behave unseemly." 1 Cor. 13:5.

    a. Courtesy is love in little things - not brutal, boisterous or hoggish.

    b. In "behaviour as becometh holiness" Tit. 2:3; 1 Tim. 3:2.

6. Unselfish - "Seeketh not her own" 1 Cor. 13:5.

    a. Man is selfish who neglects good of others. 1 Cor. 10:24; Phil. 2:4.

    b. Love is satisifed only in profit and salvation of all. 1 Cor. 10:33.

7. Good Temper - "Is not easily provoked." 1 Cor. 13:5.

    a. Temper not evil but failure to control it - blot on otherwise good character.

    b. Must be slow to anger. Prov. 16:32; Tit. 1:7; Jas. 1:19.

8. Justice - "Thinketh no evil." 1 Cor. 13:5.

    a. Puts best construction on motives and acts of others - gives benefit of doubt.

b. Passes over sins - doesn't tell everything. Prov. 10:12; 17:9; 1 Pet. 4:8.

c. Does not invent or devise evil.

9. Righteousness - "Rejoiceth not in iniquity, but in truth." 1 Cor. 13:6.

   a. Rejoices not in misfortunes of enemy - nor in wrong of any kind.

   b. The wicked rejoice is sin. Psa. 10:3; Rom. 1:32, but these in truth. 2 Jno. 4.

10. A Summary - 1 Cor. 13:7-8.

   a. "Beareth all things" - not overcome by any.

   b. "Believeth all things" - not distrustful and suspicious.

   c. "Hopeth all things" - looks for improvement in the bad.

   d. "Endureth all things" - persecution and suffering.

   e. "Never faileth" - eternal in nature.

III. Conclusion.

A. The shortest route to any good is through love.

B. Love will crown us victors - if we allow it to accompany us.

The Power Of God's Word
Heb. 4:12

I. **Introduction.**
   A. Not a dead letter - but living and active. Heb. 4:12; 1 Pet. 1:23.
   B. The devil knows there is power in it. Lk. 8:12.
   C. Even man's word has power for good and evil. Prov. 25:11; Mt. 12:36-37.
      1. Illustrate by Alexander Campbell and Robert Ingersoll.

II. **Discussion.**
   A. Miraculous Power In God's Spoken Word.
      1. Worlds made by his word. Heb. 11:3; Psa. 33:6; Gen. 1.
      2. All things upheld by word of his power. Heb. 1:3; 2 Pet. 3:7.
      3. Christ performed many miracles by his word.
         a. Stilled the raging tempest. Mt. 8:23-27.
         b. Fed great multitudes. Mt. 14:15-21.
         c. Called the dead to life. Lk. 7:11-16; 8:49-56; Jno. 11:43, 44.
      4. But this lesson concerns power of gospel.
   B. Power Shown By Comparison.
      1. Power in food to strengthen hungry. Jas. 2:15, 16; Cf. Mt. 4:4; 1 Pet. 2:2.
      2. Power in medicine to heal sick. Mt. 9:12; Cf. Psa. 107:20; Mt. 13:15.
      3. Power in light to reveal. Eph. 5:13. Cf. Psa. 119:105, 130.
         a. Note things it reveals. God, Christ, H.S. Hell, heaven, sin, way of salvation.
      4. Power in fire to destroy and purify. Lk. 17:29; Mal. 3:2; Cf. Jer. 23:29; 20:9.
      5. Power in hammer to crush. Jer. 23:29.
         a. Stony hearts must be broken. Mt. 13:15; Rom.

169

2:5; Heb. 3:12, 13.

6. Power in seed to produce fruit. Gen. 1:11; Cf. Lk. 8:11.

   a. Relate parable of the sower. Mt. 13:3-8; 18-23.

7. Power in rain to make earth fruitful. Jas. 5:7; 17, 18. Cf. Isa. 55:10, 11.

8. Power in sword to kill. Mt. 26:52. Cf. Eph. 6:17; Heb. 4:12.

C. All-Sufficiency of Its Power.

1. It is able to produce faith. Jno. 20:30, 31; Acts 15:7; Rom. 10:17.

2. It is able to make wise. 2 Tim. 3:15.

3. It is God's begetting power. Jas. 1:18; 1 Cor. 4:15.

4. The power that produces our birth. 1 Pet. 1:23.

5. The power that purifies the soul. 1 Pet. 1:22.

6. The power that converts the soul. Psa. 19:7.

7. The power that cleanses us. Jno. 15:3; Eph. 5:25-26.

8. The power that sanctifies. Jno. 17:17.

9. The power that makes us free. Jno. 8:32.

10. Able to give an inheritance. Acts 20:32.

11. It is able to save. Jas. 1:21; Rom. 1:16; Acts 11:14; 1 Cor. 15:1.

12. The power by which we will be judged. Jno. 12:48.

D. The Power May Be Resisted and Rejected.

1. God doesn't force men to accept it. Rev. 22:17; Jno. 5:40.

2. Jews resisted Holy Spirit. Acts 7:51-52.

3. False teachers resist the truth. 2 Tim. 3:8.

4. Saul rejected word of Lord. 1 Sam. 15:23.

5. Pharisees rejected commandments and counsel. Mark 7:9; Lk. 7:30.

6. How we may resist it.

   a. His word says believe (Acts 16:31) If I refuse, I resist.

   b. His word says repent (Acts 17:30) If I refuse, I resist.

   c. His word says confess (1 Jno. 4:15) If I refuse, I resist.

   d. His word says be baptized (Acts 2:38) If I refuse, I resist.

III. Conclusion.

A. All promises depend on obedience. Heb. 5:8-9.

B. To disobey insures our condemnation. 1 Pet. 4:17; 2 Thess. 1:8.

Self-Denial
Matt. 16:24

I. **Introduction.**
   A. Religion of Christ tells of difficulties to be met. Cf. Mt. 8:19, 20; Lk. 14:28-31.
   B. Self-denial is not self-destruction, but self-development.
   C. Much opposition to Christianity from those not willing to deny self.

II. **Discussion.**
   A. Importance of Self-Denial.
      1. Not an occasional act, but the ground of Christian existence. Lk. 9:23.
      2. Holiness essential to Christianity (Heb. 12:14) - no holiness without self-denial.
      3. Purity of heart essential (Mt. 5:8) - no purity of heart without self-denial.
      4. Doing God's will essential (Mt. 7:21) - impossible without self-denial. Cf. Isa. 55:7-9.
   B. Of What Must We Deny Ourselves?
      1. Sinful Pleasures.
         a. Must not be lovers nor servants of pleasures. 2 Tim. 3:4; Tit. 3:3.
         b. To live in pleasure means condemnation. 1 Tim. 5:6; Jas. 5:5.
         c. Worldly pleasures crowd out the word. Lk. 8:14.
         d. Moses an example of self-denial in this. Heb. 11:24-26.
      2. Ungodliness. Tit. 2:11-12.
         a. Ungodliness leads to perdition. 1 Pet. 4:18; 2 Pet. 3:7.
         b. Shun things that lead to ungodliness. 2 Tim. 2:16; Cf. Card parties, etc.
         c. Abstain from every form of evil. 1 Thess. 5:22.
      3. Worldly Lusts. Tit. 2:11, 12; Cf. 1 Jno. 2:15-17.

172

a. The lust of the flesh.
  (1) Make no provision for the flesh. Rom. 13:14; Gal. 5:16.
  (2) Must crucify lusts of flesh. Gal. 5:24; Rom. 8:13; Col. 3:5; 1 Pet. 2:11.
  (3) Paul an example of self-denial in this. 1 Cor. 9:27.
b. The lust of the eye. 1 Tim. 6:9.
4. Self-Exaltation.
  a. Be willing to occupy low station. Lk. 14:7-11.
  b. Don't think yourself better than others. Rom. 12:3; Phil. 2:3; 2 Cor. 10:18.
  c. Paul practiced self-denial in this. 1 Cor. 15:9; Eph. 3:8.
5. Liberties that hurt others.
  a. Don't destroy a brother to uphold your liberty. Rom. 14:15, 21; 1 Cor. 8:9, 13.
  b. Some will destroy congregations rather than sacrifice their rights.
6. Our own happiness.
  a. Self-interest antagonistic to spirit of Christianity. Rom. 15:2; 1 Cor. 10:24; Phil. 2:4.
  b. Interest in others brought Christ to earth. Rom. 15:3.
  c. Serving others as well as self should be our aims. 1 Cor. 9:22; 10:33.
7. Financial matters.
  a. Should be willing to sacrifice luxuries for gospel's sake.
  b. Rich young man unwilling to deny self. Mt. 19:16-22.
8. Relatives.
  a. Must love God more than relations. Lk. 14:26; Mt. 10:37.
  b. One disciple forbidden to bury father. Lk. 9:57-62.
9. Anything That Hinders.
  a. Even things as dear as eye, hand or foot. Mk. 9:43-48.
  b. Be willing to forsake all things. Lk. 14:33.
10. Even Life Itself.
  a. To save life is to lose it - to lose it is to save it. Mt. 16:25; Jno. 12:25.
  b. Paul placed low estimate on life. Acts 20:34;

Phil. 3:7, 8.
c. Others loved not life unto death. Rev. 12:11.

III. **Conclusion.**
A. Three attractions in text - self denial, cross, absolute surrender.
B. The motive for this - "for his sake." Mt. 16:25.
C. Christ did more than this "for our sakes." 2 Cor. 8:9.

The Free Agency Of Man
Deut 11:26

I. **Introduction.**
   A. Two theories regarding man's actions.
      1. God fore-ordained whatever comes to pass.
      2. Man is a free moral agent - responsible for own acts.

II. **Discussion.**
   A. Predestination Investigated.
      1. Arguments answered,
         a. Those ordained to eternal life believed. Acts 13:48.
            (1) Word "ordained" means "disposed." Cf. v. 46
            (2) If "foreordained," then all infants there were reprobates.
         b. "Have mercy on whom I will." Rom. 9:15, 18.
            (1) He wills mercy on the merciful. Mt. 5:7; Jas. 2:13.
            (2) Gospel either softens or hardens. 2 Cor. 2:16.
         c. Potter makes vessels to honor or dishonor. Rom. 9:21.
            (1) Vessel "married" in potter's hand. (Jer. 18:4) Not "designed" to dishonor.
            (2) Another vessel made of "less value" (Jer. 18:4) - to be used, not destroyed.
            (3) Becoming vessel of honor depends on man. 2 Tim. 2:20, 21.
         d. "From beginning chosen to salvation." 2 Thess. 2:13.
            (1) This choosing was on conditions. 2 Thess. 2:13.
         e. Certain men ordained to condemnation. Jude 4.
            (1) Characters of this nature were thus ordain-

175

ed.

2. This makes God unjust and man irresponsible.
   a. Did God foreordain the murder by Cain? Gen. 4?
   b. Did he foreordain the adultery of David? 2 Sam. 11?
   c. Did he foreordain the sin of Achan? Josh. 6.
   d. Did he foreordain the lie of Ananias and Sapphira? Acts 5.

3. It makes God the author of all evil.

B. God Desires Salvation of All.
   1. Has no pleasure in death of wicked. Ezek. 18:23, 31, 32; 33:11.
   2. Wills the salvation of all. Mt. 18:14; 1 Tim. 2:4; 2 Pet. 3:9.

C. He Grieves Over Conduct of Sinners.
   1. Repented that he made man - grieved at heart. Gen. 6:6.
   2. Grieved with Israel. 40 years. Psa. 95:10; Heb. 3:10.
   3. They vexed him by rebellion. Isa. 63:10.
   4. "O, that thou hadst hearkened." Isa. 48:18.
   5. Jesus wept over Jerusalem. Lk. 13:34; 19:41, 42.

D. Man Addressed As A Free Agent.
   1. Blessing and curse, life and death set before him. Deut. 11:26-28; 30:15.
   2. "Choose whom you will serve." Josh. 24:15.
   3. "Come unto me - give you rest." Mt. 11:28-30.
   4. "If any man will come after me." Mt. 16:24.
   5. "Ye will not come." Jno. 5:40.
   6. "Whosoever will, let him come." Rev. 22:17; Jno. 7:37.

E. Man's Conduct Determines His Standing.
   1. We choose the master we serve. Josh. 24:15; Jno. 8:34; Rom. 6:16.
   2. Salvation depends on obedience.
      a. Remission of sins and eternal salvation. Rom. 6:17; Heb. 5:8-9.
      b. Entrance to heaven on conditions. Mt. 7:21; Rev. 22:14.
   3. Condemnation the reward of disobedience.
      a. Condemned because believe not. Jno. 3:18, 36.
      b. Destruction and anguish to disobedient. 2 Thess. 1:8, 9; Rom. 2:8, 9; Eph. 5:6.

III. Conclusion.

A. Darkey's idea of election - Devil votes *against* you, God votes *for* you, you vote *for* yourself.

B. Make calling and election sure. 2 Pet. 1:10.

Christian Stewardship
1 Pet. 4:10

I. **Introduction.**
   A. Steward defined: "One having charge of another's possession."
   B. Stewardship embraces service: "Minister one to another." 1 Pet. 4:10.
   C. Nothing more glorified in Bible than service.
      1. By service we imitate Christ and keep his memory fresh to world.

II. **Discussion.**
   A. Why We Are Stewards.
      1. Were bought with a price. 1 Cor. 6:19, 20; 1 Pet. 1:18, 19.
      2. Gave ourselves willingly to God. 2 Cor. 8:5; Rom. 6:16.
   B. Stewards of "Manifold" Grace.
      1. The Grace of time.
         a. Some have no time for Lord - time for business, pleasure, etc.
         b. Must redeem the time. Eph. 5:16; Col. 4:5.
         c. Night comes when none can work. Jno. 9:4.
         d. Failure in this will mean condemnation. Jer. 8:20; Mt. 25:1-13.
      2. The Grace of influence.
         a. We are bound to exert influence of some nature.
         b. Let not good be evilly spoken of. Rom. 14:15.
         c. Must let light shine. Mt. 5:16; 1 Pet. 2:12.
      3. The Grace of ability.
         a. Paul recognized difference of ability. 1 Cor. 12:14-22; Rom. 12:4-8.
         b. If prophecy-according to proportion of faith (This required inspiration).
         c. If ministry (service) - wait on it. Rom. 12:7.
            (1) The seven were chosen to give attention to

178

service. Acts 6:1-3.

    (2) Deacons must "use" the office. 1 Tim. 3:10, 11.

  d. If teaching - give attention to it. Rom. 12:7.

    (1) Elders were to be "apt to teach." 1 Tim. 3:2;

    (2) Gospel committed to our stewardship. 1 Cor. 4:1, 2; 2 Tim. 2:2; 1 Thess. 2:4; 1 Tim. 1:11.

    (3) Ability to teach may be natural or acquired.

  e. If exhortation - give attention to it. Rom. 12:18.

    (1) Timothy was commanded to exhort. 1 Tim. 4:13; 2 Tim. 4:2.

    (2) We should exhort each other. Heb. 3:13; 10:25.

  f. If giving - with liberality. Rom. 12:8.

    (1) The earth is the Lord's. 1 Cor. 10:25; Ezek. 16:17; 1 Chron. 29:14-16.

    (2) Give according to ability. 1 Cor. 16:1-2; 2 Cor. 8:12-14; 1 Pet. 4:11.

    (3) Give liberally and cheerfully. 2 Cor. 9:6-7.

    (4) Ill. "Darkies giving by 3 rules, give something; according to ability; willingly.

  g. If ruling - with diligence (careful attention and effort) Rom. 12:8.

    (1) Eldership is a stewardship. Tit. 1:7.

    (2) Watch for souls of those under them. Heb. 13:17.

  h. If showing mercy - with cheerfulness. Rom. 12:8.

    (1) All can show mercy in some way. Mt. 5:7.

    (2) God loves a cheerful giver. 2 Cor. 9:7.

  i. Responsibility based on ability. Mt. 25:14; Lk. 12:41-48.

C. Faithfulness Required.

  1. Required that a steward be found faithful. 1 Cor. 4:2.

    a. Apply to preceding points of stewardship.

  2. The parable of the unjust steward. Lk. 16:1-12.

    a. He had wasted his lord's goods. vs. 1.

      (1) We may waste time, unfluences, ability, money, etc.

    b. Note his wisdom in making friends. v. 2-7.

      (1) His wisdom, not his dishonesty, was commended. v. 8.

    c. Make God and Christ our friends. Of (by) mammon of unrighteousness. v. 9.

d. In faithful in little, faithful in much, etc. v. 10.

III. Conclusion.
A. All are trusted with Lord's goods in some department.
B. Should ask: "Am I a good steward?"
C. Should ever strive to be better stewards.

Contend For The Faith
Jude 3

I. Introduction.
A. It was "needful" for Jude to exhort them. v. 3.
B. This need arose from work of false teachers. v. 4.
C. We are in an age of indifference, insincerity and false teachers.
D. Jude's exhortation very needful today.

II. Discussion.
A. What is "The Faith?"
   1. Faith sometimes means belief. Jno. 20:27; Rom. 4:20; Heb. 11:6.
   2. It sometimes means fidelity. Rom. 1:8; 1 Thess. 1:8.
   3. In text it refers to the gospel (system of faith).
      a. It is something that was delivered. Jude 3. Cf. 1 Cor. 15:1-4.
      b. Something that was revealed. Gal. 3:23-25; Cf. 1 Pet. 1:10-12.
      c. Something that was preached. Gal. 1:23; Cf. Rom. 10:8.
      d. It could be obeyed. Acts 6:7; Rom. 1:5.
      e. Could be established in it. Acts 16:5; Col. 1:23; 1 Cor. 16:13.
      f. May be departed from. 1 Tim. 4:1; 6:10.
      g. Should be contended for. Jude 5; Phil. 1:27.
B. The Meaning of "Contend."
   1. No authority for contention and strife toward each other. Phil. 1:15, 16.
   2. But rather a defense of the gospel. Phil. 1, 7, 17.
   3. When gospel is assailed, stand up for it.
   4. This may be done by argument and dispute.
      a. Stephen successfully disputed with adversaries. Acts 6:9-10.
      b. Paul disputed with the Grecians. Acts 9:29.
      c. He defended the faith against Elymas. Acts

13:6-13.
- d. Paul and Barnabas disputed with Judaizing teachers. Acts 15:1, 2.
- e. Paul disputed daily in market at Athens. Acts 17:17.
- f. Also daily for 2 years in school of Tyrannus. Acts 19:9-10.

5. Not only defend, but make gospel aggressive.

C. "Earnestly" Contend.

1. Whatever we do should be with our might. Eccl. 9:10.

2. Should "boldly" declare the gospel. Acts 4:29; Eph. 6:19, 20; 1 Thess. 2:2; Phil. 1:14.

D. Once Delivered.

1. Revised version: "Once for all delivered."

2. Revelation has thus been completed.
- a. Jesus the author and finisher of our (Gr. the) faith. Heb. 12:2.
- b. Revelation made by the Spirit. 1 Cor. 2:9, 10; Eph. 3:3-5.
- c. But all the truth was revealed. Jno. 14:26; 16:13.
- d. Forbidden to preach another gospel. Gal. 1:8, 9.
- e. It is a perfect system. Jas. 1:25; Cf. 1 Cor. 13:9, 10.
- f. Contains all things pertaining to life and godliness. 2 Pet. 1:3.

3. Those who claim new revelations todays are impostors.
- a. Various revelations (?) received about end of world.
- b. Revealed to girl at Springfield, Mo. to teach me I was wrong.
- c. Book of Mormon claimed as divine revelation.

E. Delivered to Saints.

1. First delivered to apostles. Mt. 28:19; Mk. 16:15, 16; Lk. 24:46-47.

2. Committed to faithful men. 2 Tim. 2:2.

3. Saints have obeyed gospel - in church of Christ. 1 Cor. 1:2.
- a. Show terms in plan of salvation.

4. New revelations claimed by those who have not obeyed these - not saints.

182

III. Conclusion.

A. Should not contend for our opinions.

B. Neither for the various doctrines of men.

C. Contend for things only that are revealed in the faith.

Walking By Faith
2 Cor. 5:7

I. **Introduction.**
   A. Christianity a system of faith. Rom. 3:27; 10:8; Gal. 1:23.
   B. Not a walk by sight.
      1. Never saw God (Ex. 33:20-22; Jno. 1:18) Christ (1 Cor. 15:8); Holy Spirit; resurrection; heaven; hell.
   C. Infidels reject Christianity because of this.
      1. But farming is a matter of faith - also other vocations.
      2. Work of Columbus and Washington matters of faith.

II. **Discussion.**
   A. Distinction Between Faith and Opinion.
      1. Faith requires evidence (Rom. 10:17; Jno. 20:30, 31) Opinion what we think.
      2. Earth "without form" faith (Gen. 1:2) How long? - opinion.
      3. "Three of knowledge" - faith (Gen. 2:9); What was it? - Opinion.
      4. Samson caught 300 foxes - faith (Judges 15:1-5); How? - opinion.
      5. Nicodemus came to Christ by night - faith (Jno. 3:2) Why by night? - Opinion.
      6. Jesus wrote on ground - faith (Jno. 8:1-11.) What? Opinion.
   B. Old Testament Examples.
      1. The first sacrifice. Gen. 4:1-5.
         a. Able walked by faith. Heb. 11:4.
         b. Cain walked by opinion. 1 Jno. 3:12.
      2. Building of Ark. Gen. 6.
         a. Noah walked by faith. Heb. 11:7; Gen. 6:22 - had he changed plans, opinion.
         b. Those who perished walked by opinion - didn't

think flood would come.

3. Walls of Jericho. Josh. 6:3-5; Heb. 11:30.
    a. Every step around was a step by faith.
4. Naaman's Leprosy. 2 Kings 5:1-14.
    a. His opinion about how it would be done. v. 11.
    b. His opinion about other rivers. v. 12.
5. Nadab and Abihu. Lev. 10:1-3.
    a. Faith required:
        (1) Take a censer.
        (2) Take fire.
        (3) Take incense.
        (4) Put incense on fire.
        (5) But fire must come from alter. Leb. 16:12-13.
    b. What they did:
        (1) Took censer.
        (2) Took fire.
        (3) Took incense.
        (4) Put incense on fire.
        (5) But offered strange fire.
C. New Testament Lessons.
    1. Baptism by burial. Rom. 6:3, 4; Col. 2:12, 13.
        a. Examples show the same. Mt. 3:16; Acts 8:36f.
        b. No evidence for sprinkling, pouring or trine immersion - opinion.
    2. Baptism of believers. Acts 8:12, 37.
        a. Infant baptism by opinion.
    3. Lord's day worship.
        a. Every first day-faith (Acts 20:7; Heb. 10:25; 1 Cor. 16:1, 2); occasionally, opinion.
D. Things Right Within Themselves, Wrong Religiously.
    1. In own affairs, may do as we please - if violate no principle of right.
    2. Not so in religion - must act by authority of Christ. Col. 3:17.
    3. The principle demonstrated.
        a. Washing vessels.
            (1) Wrong not to wash them - uncleanliness.
            (2) To wash them as religious service wrong - not of faith. Mark. 7:4, 7-9.
        b. Eating meat.
            (1) Not wrong within itself. Rom. 14:2, 3; 1 Tim. 4:3, 4.
            (2) Wrong on Lord's table - not of faith.
        c. Instrumental music.

185

(1) Not wrong within itself.

(2) Wrong as religious worship - not of faith. Eph. 5:19.

III. Conclusion.

A. Doing what God says makes men of faith. Heb. 11.

B. What he says worth more than our opinions.

C. Divine worship intended to please God - not meet man's fancies.

Who Shall Be Able To Stand?
Rev. 6:17

I. **Introduction.**
   A. Views regarding text.
      1. Day of final judgment of world - points correspond. Mt. 24:29-31.
      2. But it's in 6th seal - commotions and upheavels in Roman Empire.
   B. Yet a great day of judgment is coming. Heb. 9:27; 10:27; 2 Pet. 2:4; Jude 6, 14, 15; Acts 17:31.
   C. This question is suitable to apply to that.

II. **Discussion.**
   A. Necessity of a Standard.
      1. No text without a standard.
         a. Legal proceedings - court decisions and legal documents.
         b. Standards of measurements - length, capacity, weight, money.
      2. Bible standard at judgment Jno. 12:48; Rev. 20:11, 12; Mt. 24:35.
   B. All Tested Even In This Life.
      1. Shown by division necessitated by gospel. Lk. 12:51-53; Mt. 10:34-36.
      2. Text for sinners.
         a. Rich young man. Mt. 19:16-22.
         b. Ruth in giving up her gods. Ruth 1:16, 17.
         c. Must forsake all to be his disciple. Lk. 14:26f.
      3. Test for children of God.
         a. The example of Job = stood the text.
         b. Abraham in offering Isaac. Gen. 22:1-12 - proved his faith.
         c. Elijah in his stand for God. 1 King 19:1-18.
         d. Three Hebrew children. Dan. 3:1-18.
         e. Christ was tested. Mt. 4:1-11.
         f. These tests for our good. Heb. 12:10, 11.

C. Why The Day Is Great. Jude 6.
 1. Some say "great" means longer - possible 1000 yrs.
 2. July 4th great - not longer - but great events associated with it.
 3. Some of the events that make the judgment day great.
    a. End of time. 2 Pet. 3:10-13.
    b. Great transaction - resurrection. Jno. 5:28, 29.
    c. Great changes - each to his destiny.
D. Who Will Stand.
 1. All will stand there, but not all stand the test.
 2. Not unbelievers. Jno. 3:18; Heb. 11:6; Lk. 12:46.
 3. Not the impenitent. Acts 17:30-31; Lk. 13:3; Rom. 2:5.
 4. Not the unbaptized. Jno. 3:5; Mk. 16:16; Acts 2:38.
 5. Not the unbaptized. Jno. 3:5; Mk. 16:16; Acts 2:38.
 6. Not backsliders or apostates. 2 Pet. 2:20, 21; Psa. 9:17; Heb. 6:4-6.
 7. Not the disobedient. Heb. 5:8, 9; 2 Thess. 1:8, 9; Mt. 7:21.
 8. Only one class will stand - the faithful. Mt. 24:12, 13; Rev. 2:10; 14:13.
E. Results of The Test.
 1. Eternal woe to those who fail. Mt. 25:46; Rev. 14:9-11; 20:10.
 2. Endless bliss to those who pass. Mt. 5:12; 2 Cor. 4:17; Rom. 8:16, 17; Rev. 21:4.

III. **Conclusion.**
A. Men prepare the examinations here - why not there?
B. No such test as that ever faced - the final test of character.
C. What will you say on that great day? What will your answer be?
D. It may depend upon your answer now.

Come And See — Go And Tell
Mt. 26:6, 7

I. **Introduction.**
  A. Easter one time in King James version (Acts 12:4) - mistranslation.
  B. Easter on 1st Sunday after 1st full moon after vernal equinox (from Mar. 22 to April 25) Pagan tribute to god of Spring.
  C. People more concerned about days God didn't authorize than those he did.
  D. Relate circumstances of the text - proof of divine Christ.

II. **Discussion.**
  A. Scriptures Challenge Investigation.
    1. Its history proves them divine.
       a. Human history inaccurate - Divine history true.
       b. Carries us beyond the pyramids or Herodotus the father of human history.
       c. Men have searched for faults.
          (1) "Flood never occurred" - but see shells found on top of mts.
          (2) "Babylon never existed" - but her ruins may yet be seen.
          (3) "Joseph lived in fiction" - but remains of irrigation works bear his name and records found showing Nile failed to overflow 7 yrs.
          (4) "Pharoah never lived" - but mummified body recently found.
          (5) "Joshua and sun a myth" - but nearly all nations have record of long day.
    2. Its prophecy infallible proof.
       a. Concerning Babylon. Isa. 13:17-22; Jer. 51: - Note some details.
       b. God's promise to Abraham. Gen. 12:1-3.
       c. Destruction of Jerusalem. Lk. 21:20-24.
       d. Many prophecies concerning Christ.

189

B. Jesus Is The Son of God.
1. He claimed to be God's son. Jno. 16:28.
2. God declared him to be. Mt. 3:17; 17:1-5.
3. Devils declared him to be. Mt. 8:29.
4. Enemies said he was. Mt. 27:54; 28:11-15.
5. Yet whole thing depended on his resurrection. 1 Cor. 15:14-19.
   a. "Our preaching otherwise, is vain" vs. 14: Cf. 1 Cor. 15:1-4.
   b. "Your faith is also vain." v. 14; Cf. Jno. 20:30, Rom. 10:17.
   c. "We are false witnesses" v. 15: Cf. Acts 1:8.
   d. "You are yet in sin." v. 17: Cf. Jno. 8:32.
   e. "Those fallen asleep have perished." v. 18; Cf. Acts 7:60.
   f. Of all men most miserable." v. 19. Cf. Matt. 5:11, 12.

C. The Empty Grave - Come and see.
1. Five things admitted by all.
   a. Jesus lived.
   b. At time ascribed.
   c. Put to death.
   d. Buried in tomb.
   e. On third day body was missing.
2. The disputed question - What became of his body?
3. Enemies evidence - "Disciples stole body." Mt. 28:11-15.
   a. Testified to a thing they were to prevent. Mt. 27:63-66.
   b. Never told it if true - their lives at stake if they went to sleep.
   c. Not competent to testify if asleep.
4. Testimony of friends. "he arose." Acts 1:21-22; 3:14, 15; 5:29-31; 10:39-41.
   a. They were not deceived - well acquainted. Acts 1:21-22; 1:1-3; Jno. 20:24-29.
   b. Not deceivers - would not have suffered for a fraud. Cf. 2 Cor. 11:23-28.
   7c. Hence, their testimony is true.

D. Go And Tell.
1. Demands proclamation. Mt. 28:19; Mk. 16:15.
2. Needed by all - only solution of worlds problems.

E. Go Quickly.
1. Millions today have never heard it.

190

2. Woman of Samaria hurried to tell friends. Jno. 4:28-29.

III. Conclusion.
A. As you have learned the story, tell others.
B. Jesus died and rose again for us. Rom. 4:25.
C. We should live and die for him.

The Christian Race
Heb. 12:1

I. **Introduction.**

   A. May derive profitable lessons from common occurances.

   B. Christian life often compared to fight, wrestle, race.

   C. Some features connected with ancient races.

      a. Race course was plainly marked out.

      b. Contestants went through system of exercise and preparations.

      c. Vast concourse of spectators assembled.

      d. Rules publicly proclaimed by heralds.

      e. Judges appointed to award the prize.

II. **Discussion.**

   A. The Race Course.

     1. Not left to prescribe for self - must keep to course.

     2. Must enter course to run. Cf. Mt. 7:13-14.

     3. How enter: faith, repentance, confession, baptism.

   B. Preparing To Run.

     1. Stenuous preparation in ancient races - we must prepare.

       a. By obeying the truth. Gal. 5:7.

       b. By forgetting the past. Phil. 3:13.

       c. By laying aside every weight. Heb. 12:1.

   C. The Witnesses.

     1. Compassed about by could of witnesses. Heb. 12:1.

     2. Apostles spectacle to world, angels and men. 1 Cor. 4:9.

     3. Our neighbors are watching our profession and practice.

     4. Heavenly eyes are watching us. Cf. Lk. 15:10.

     5. Inspiration to ancient runner that countrymen were watching.

       a. It widened the glory of victory - deepened shame of defeat.

D. Rules Governing Race.
   1. Must strive lawfully. 2 Tim. 2:5.
   2. Must not establish own righteousness. Rom. 10:3; Heb. 12:14.
   3. An empty profession will not do. Tit. 1:16.
   4. Some rules to observe.
      a. With patience Heb. 12:1.
      b. With temperance. 1 Cor. 9:25.
      c. With Zeal. Phil. 3:14.
      d. Look unto Jesus. Heb. 12:2.
E. The Judge.
   1. Lord is the judge. Jno. 5:22, 27; Acts 10:42; 17:31; 2 Tim. 4:7, 8.
   2. Will reward as we deserve. Rev. 20:11-12.
F. Wherein The Races Differ.
   1. In the reward.
      a. Little profit (1 Tim. 4:8) Crown of leaves - corruptible. Cf. 1 Cor. 9:25.
      b. Our crown described. 2 Tim. 4:7, 8; Jas. 1:12; 1 Pet. 5:4; 1:4.
   2. In number of victors.
      a. Only one could receive the prize. 1 Cor. 9:24, 26.
      b. All who run lawfully in Christian race can win. 1 Cor. 9:26.
   3. In Consequences to non-participants.
      a. Those who did not run suffered no disadvantage.
      b. Will be called to account if we fail to enter race. Mt. 22:5; 7:26-27.
   4. In results to those who fail.
      a. They lost only their labor or were humiliated - no punishment.
      b. But we must persevere or be condemned. 1 Cor. 9:24; Mt. 10:22; Heb. 10:38; 2 Pet. 2:20, 21; Phil. 3:14.

III. Conclusion.
A. If told to run for life, we would make haste.
B. The souls are more valuable, the consequences more terrible.
C. But the race must be run in this life.

The Truth Makes Free
Jno. 8:32

I. **Introduction.**
   A. This spoken to rebellious Jews.
   B. Its principle needs restressing today.
   C. The world is sadly in need of the truth.
   D. But often, like these Jews ,they don't realize it. Cf. vs. 33.

II. **Discussion.**
   A. What Is The Truth?
      1. "Truth" may refer to anything that is true.
      2. But in text it refers to gospel. Jno. 17:17.
         a. It may be turned away from. 2 Tim. 4:3, 4; Tit. 1:14; Jas. 5:19.
         b. Something that may be obeyed. 1 Pet. 1:22, 23.
         c. The system brought by Christ. Jno. 1:17.
         d. Gospel called "word, of truth." Eph. 1:13; Col. 1:5; Jno. 17:17; 2 Tim. 2:15; Jas. 1:18.
   B. Bondage Implied.
      1. Illustrate bondage by african slavery.
      2. Also by bondage of Israel in Egypt. Ex. 1:7-14.
      3. These were in the bondage of sin. Jno. 8:33-34; Cf. Rom. 6:17, 20; 2 Pet. 2:19.
      4. Sinners bound by the cords of sin. Prov. 5:22; Acts 8:23.
      5. Taken captive is snare of devil. 2 Tim. 2:25-26.
      6. Bondage of sin the worst of all bondage - result.
   C. Liberty Offered.
      1. Shall be made free indeed. Jno. 8:36; Rom. 6:14.
      2. Gospel is called "law of liberty." Jas. 1:25; 2:12.
      3. Makes free from law of sin and death. Rom. 8:2; Gal. 5:1.
      4. Freedom from sin the greatest of all liberty.
      5. Liberty does not mean "do as you please." Gal. 5:13; 1 Pet. 2:16.

194

D. Must Know The Truth.
  1. God wants all to know it. 1 Tim. 2:4.
  2. Had it revealed that we might know. Jno. 14:26; 16:13.
  3. Commanded that it should be taught. Mt. 28:19; 2 Tim. 2:2.
  4. It must be heard. Jno. 6:45; Rom. 10:14, 17.
  5. To know it is to understand it.
      a. Those who fail to understand, not converted. Mt. 13:15; Eph. 4:18.
      b. Good-ground-hearer understood. Mt. 13:23.
      c. Philip asked: "Understandest what thou readest?
      d. Gospel addressed to man's understanding (Heb. 8:10, 11) hence infants not included.
E. Knowledge Implies Obedience.
  1. Professing to know without obedience unprofitable. Tit. 1:16; 1 Jno. 2:4.
  2. Must obey truth to be made free. 1 Pet. 1:22; Rom.
  3. Conditions on which freedom depends.
      a. Without faith will die in sin. Jno. 9:24; Cf. Heb. 11:6.
      b. Repentance helps to recover from captivity. 2 Tim. 5:25, 26. Cf. Lk. 13:3; Acts 3:19.
      c. Confession leads to deliverance. Rom. 10:9, 10.
      d. Made free when baptized. Rom. 6:17, 18. Cf. Rom. 6:3, 4; Acts 2:38; 22:16.
  4. It is "the truth" - not error - that makes free.

III. Conclusion.
A. The truth shall never fail. 1 Pet. 1:23, 25.
B. Yet men may resist the truth. 2 Tim. 3:8.
C. They must suffer if they do. Rom. 2:8, 9.

The Conquest Over Temptation
1 Cor. 10:13

I. **Introduction.**
   A. Paul had referred to Israel's deliverance. v. 1-4.
   B. Relates their overthrow in wilderness.
   1. Idolaters. v. 7; Ex. 32:6.
   2. Fornicators. v. 8; Num. 25:1.
   3. Tempted Christ. v. 9; Num. 21:6.
   4. Murmurers. v. 10.
   C. All this history for our example. v. 11.
   D. Shows danger of falling. v. 12 - but thought arises, why need they fall? v. 13.

II. **Discussion.**
   A. Certainty of Encountering Temptation.
   1. None ever lived above it - David, Solomon, Moses, etc.
   2. If Christ tempted, mortal men not exempt. Cf. Jno. 15:20; Heb. 4:15.
   3. More active we become, more active devil becomes.
   B. Sources of Temptation. 1 Jno. 2:16, 17; 2 Pet. 2:18.
   1. These were used in Eden. Gen. 3:6.
   2. Also used against Christ. Mt. 4:1-11.
   3. Satan back of all temptation. Jas. 1:13-15; 1 Thess. 3:5.
   C. Our Strength.
   1. Like chains - no stronger than weakest link.
   2. Satan hunts our weak points.
      a. After 40 day fast, struck at appetite. Mt. 4:3.
      b. Christ worshipful - tempted to worship. Mt. 4:9.
      c. Covetous tempted with riches. 1 Tim. 6:9, 10.
   D. No Temptation Insurmountable.
   1. Only such as "common to man." (Text.)
   2. "Common to man" - moderate - a way of escape. 2 Pet. 2:9.

3. "God is faithful" (text) - Cf. 1 Thess. 5:23, 24; 2 Thess. 3:3.
4. But we must do the escaping. 1 Cor. 10:14.

E. How To Escape.
   1. By avoiding temptation.
      a. "Refrain foot from their path." Prov. 1:10-15.
      b. "Enter not into path of wicked." Prov. 4:14-15.
      c. "Abstain from all appearance of evil." 1 Thess. 5:22.
      d. If we willingly approach sin, we tempt the devil.
      e. If your work bares weak points to devil, better change.
   2. By whipping the devil.
      a. Easy to "whip devil around the stump" - but what of face to face battle?
      b. Can devil be whipped? Cf. Mt. 4:11.
      c. We must resist him. Jas. 4:7; 1 Pet. 5:9.
      d. Give him no place. Eph. 4:27.
      e. Be arrayed in whole armor. Eph. 6:11.
      f. We have same weapon Jesus used. "It is written."

G. Some Points To Be Guarded.
   1. If tempted to revenge "It is written." Rom. 12:17-21.
   2. If tempted to steal - "It is written." Eph. 4:28.
   3. If tempted to pride. "It is written." Jas. 4:6.
   4. If tempted to hate - "It is written." 1 Jno. 3:15.
   5. If tempted to worldliness - "It is written." 1 Jno. 2:15.
   6. If tempted to gossip - "It is written." Tit. 3:2.
   7. If tempted to blaspheme - "It is written." Col. 3:2.
   8. If tempted to stay home or visit on Lord's day - "It is written." Heb. 10:25.

III. Conclusion.
A. Temptation not sin - "yielding is sin."
B. We should have the courage of Joseph. Gen. 39:7-12.
C. "Each victory will help us some other to win."
D. "To him that overcometh, God giveth a crown." Jas. 1:12.

The Reason Of Our Hope
1 Pet. 3:15

I. **Introduction.**

   A. Solomon sought the reason of things. Eccl. 7:25.

   B. Men who can render a reason, seldom conceited. Cf. 26:16.

   C. Are told to prove all things. 1 Thess. 5:21.

   D. Should know how to answer every man. Col. 4:6.

   E. Give answer for reason of our hope. (Text.)

II. **Discussion.**

   A. What The Hope In Us?

      1. The hope of the resurrection. Acts 23:6; 24:15; 26:6-8; 1 Thess. 4:14-18.

      2. The hope of salvation. 1 Thess. 5:8; Rom. 8:24, 25.

      3. Hope of eternal life. Tit. 1:2; 3:7.

      4. Hope of being like Christ. 1 Jno. 3:2, 3.

   B. Be Ready To Answer.

      1. Paul was ready to preach at Rome. Rom. 1:15.

      2. Elders should teach with ready mind. 1 Pet. 5:2.

      3. All should be ready to give answer when asked. (Text).

         a. "Ready" implies willingness. Cf. 1 Tim. 6:18; 1 Pet. 5:2.

         b. Also implies ability.

            (1) Elders should be able to defend gospel. Tit. 1:9.

            (2) Paul rebuked those not able to give reason. Heb. 5:12-14.

      4. All this implies knowledge of Bible. Rom. 15:4; 1 Cor. 1:23; 2 Tim. 2:15; 3:15.

   C. Reasons Often Given.

      1. Like a certain good man.

         a. Suppose that man was mistaken?

         b. Must not so compare ourselves. 2 Cor. 10:12.

      2. Am satisfied with my religion.

  a. Things not always what they seem. Prov. 14:12.

  b. Can I afford to be satisifed with less than satisifies God?

 3. I have a clear conscience.

  a. Conscience not a guide - Cf. Hindu religion.

  b. Saul lived in all good conscience. Acts 23:1; 24:16; 26:9.

 4. Feel it in my heart.

  a. Heart is not in left side. Eccl. 10:2.

  b. It is also deceitful. Jer. 17:9; Prov. 28:26.

 5. Am living a moral life.

  a. Cornelius not saved on morality. Acts 10.

  b. Must work in vineyard. Mt. 20:1.

D. A Scriptural Answer.

 1. "Because we love the brethren." 1 Jno. 3:14.

  a. Who are the brethren. Mt. 12:47-50.

  b. How we know we love them. 1 Jno. 5:2. Cf. 1 Jno. 2:3, 4.

 2. Commandments to be obeyed.

  a. Faith. Acts 16:31.

  b. Repentance. Acts 17:30.

  c. Confession. Rom. 10:9-10.

  d. Baptism. Acts 10:48.

  e. Faithfulness. Rev. 2:10.

E. Why Rely On Scripture?

 1. "No contradictions" prove its divinity.

 2. Fulfilled prophecy an infallible proof.

 3. Its continued existence despite opposition.

III. Conclusion.

A. Should be able to answer every man - friend or foe.

B. Should answer with meekness and fear.

C. Can't afford to accept anything less than scripture.

Draw Near To God
Jas. 4:8

I. **Introduction.**
  A. Nearness not geographical fact - may live close geographically, yet far apart; or vice versa.
  B. Text indicates we may be away from God.
  C. Sin is that which separates. Isa. 59:1, 2.
  D. But we have the ability to draw near to him.

II. **Discussion.**
  A. The One Near Whom We Draw.
    1. He is an omnipotent being. Gen. 18:14; Job 42:2; Rev. 19:6.
      a. Should desire to be near an all-powerful being.
    2. He is an omnipresent being. 1 Kgs. 8:27; Psa. 139:7-10; Jer. 23:24.
      a. Should want to be near one in whose presence we are bound to be.
    3. He is an omniscient being. Psa. 147:5; Heb. 4:13.
      a. Should desire to be near one who knows all we do.
    4. He is willing to be approached. 2 Pet. 3:9.
  B. Means Of Drawing Near.
    1. To the sinner.
      a. Must come through Christ. Jno. 14:6; Eph. 2:18; Heb. 7:25.
      b. By the blood of Christ. Eph. 2:13.
      c. According to God's will. Heb. 10:9, 10; 7:19.
    2. To the child of God.
      a. Israel drew near in tabernacle service.
        (1) God was nigh unto them. Deut. 4:7.
        (2) Even dwelt among them. Ex. 25:8; Lev. 26:11, 12.
      b. Christians must come with true hearts. Heb. 10:22; Jas. 4:8; Cf. Psa. 34:18.
      c. We draw near in song. Eph. 5:19; Col. 3:16; 1

Cor. 14:15.

      (1) Song service no time for conversation.

    d. We draw near in prayer. Heb. 13:15.

      (1) Lord nigh to them that call. Psa. 145:18.

      (2) Come boldly to throne of grace. Heb. 4:16.

      (3) Should serve God with reverence. Heb. 12:28, Cf. whispering during prayer.

    e. We draw near in Lord's supper.

      (1) A memorial of solemn event. 1 Cor. 11:23-26.

      (2) A communion (participation) of body and blood. 1 Cor. 11:16.

      (3) Must have mind on Lord's body. 1 Cor. 11:29.

    f. Draw near in daily godly living - cleanse hands purify hearts (text).

C. We May Draw Away.

    1. Draw near with lips - heart far away. Mt. 15:8.

    2. Displeased with them that draw back. Heb. 10:38, 39.

    3. Draw back when we rebel against any commandment - baptism, assembly, contribution, purity, etc.

D. How Near Should We Come?

    1. Nearer than in nature. Acts 17:27.

    2. Near enough to be friends. Jas. 2:23.

    3. Near enough to be children. 2 Cor. 6:18.

    4. Near enough to be one. Jno. 17:21.

E. Results of Drawing Near.

    1. It is good for us. Psa. 73:28; 65:4.

    2. We find grace and mercy. Heb. 4:16.

    3. God will draw near to us. Jas. 4:8.

    4. Nearness leads to resemblance. 1 Cor. 15:33; Cf. Acts 4:13.

III. Conclusion.

A. Christ came to draw men to himself. Jno. 12:32.

B. We should delight to approach God. Isa. 58:2.

C. Intimacy with God rests with us.

Reconciliation
2 Cor. 5:20

I. **Introduction.**
  A. Reconciliation defined: "Re" - again - "conciliation" - to make friends.
  B. Implies parties once friends - now estranged.
  1. Both may be equal - or one superior, other inferior.
  2. Both may be guilty - or one innocent, other guilty.
  C. Mediator usually necessary to bring about reconciliation.

II. **Discussion.**
  A. A Mediator.
  1. Easy to find if both the estranged are equal - hard if unequal.
  2. Easy to find if both are guilty - hard if only one.
  3. Requirements of a mediator (apply to reconciliation of men).
      a. Must not be party to the difference.
      b. Must be adapted to both parties - high or low.
      c. Must bear same relation to each - otherwise partial.
      d. Must become acquainted with all facts leading to trouble.
      e. His decision is final.
  B. God And Man Estranged.
  1. Man responsible for the estrangement - he is guilty; God, innocent.
      a. God forsook Israel at Ai because of sin. Josh. 7:11-12.
      b. Sin separated man from God. Isa. 59:1, 2; 64:7.
      c. Alienated by wicked works. Col. 1:21; Eph. 4:18.
  2. Man must be reconciled to God, not God to man. 2 Cor. 5:19-20.
  C. Our Mediator.
  1. Only Christ is qualified. 1 Tim. 2:5; 2 Cor. 5:18, 19;

Heb. 2:17.

    a. Man meets no requirements of mediator (apply to each of above).

    b. Angels cannot be - not equal with God, nor lowly.

  2. Christ only is qualified. 1 Tim. 2:5; 2 Cor. 5:18, 19; Heb. 2:17.

    a. Not a party to the difference. 2 Cor. 5:21; 1 Pet. 2:22.

    b. Adapted to both parties. Phil. 2:6-8.

    c. Related to both - Diety the father. Mt. 1:20; Lk. 1:35; humanity the mother. Gen. 3:15; Mt. 1:23.

      (1) If wholly divine, or wholly human, would not do.

    d. Acquainted with all facts leading to difficulty - was in the beginning. Jno. 1:1, 2.

D. Means of Reconciliation.

  1. Every mediator must use some means to effect friendship.

  2. The means Christ used.

    a. He shed his blood. Rom. 5:10; Eph. 2:12-16; Col. 1:20.

      (1) Effect of his death - universalists say all, Unitarians say none - truth between.

    b. By ministry of apostles. 2 Cor. 5:18, 20; Jno. 20:23; Mt. 16:19.

    c. By the word. 2 Cor. 5:19.

E. Where Reconciliation Takes Place.

  1. Takes place in Christ. 2 Cor. 5:19.

  2. Or in the one body. Eph. 2:16; Cf. Eph. 1:22, 23.

F. The Conditions Imposed.

  1. The innocent party has right to make condition.

  2. The condition made known through mediator.

    a. Must believe gospel. Acts 16:31.

    b. Must repent of sins. Acts 17:30.

    c. Must confess Christ. Mt. 10:32; 1 Jno. 4:15.

    d. Must be baptized. Acts 2:38; 22:16.

  3. As reconciliation occurs in Christ, show that these bring into him. Rom. 10:10; Acts 11:18; Gal. 3:27.

III. Conclusion.

A. God desires all to be reconciled. 1 Tim. 2:4.

B. Promises pardon if we comply. Heb. 8:12; Rom. 5:10; 2 Cor. 5:19.

C. Both rejoice when reconciliation effected. Lk. 15:7; Rom. 5:11.

Things That Hinder
Gal. 5:7

I. **Introduction.**

    A. Hindrances in all walks of life - farmer, merchant, painter, etc.

    B. Great things could be accomplished if nothing hindered.

    C. In Christianity may run well for awhile - then be hindered. Gal. 5:7.

    D. In view of results, should strive to overcome hindrances.

II. **Discussion.**

    A. The source of Hindrances.

        1. Not from him that called us. Gal. 5:8.

            a. The Lord strengthens us. Phil. 4:13; 1 Pet. 5:10.

            b. He is our helper - not hinderer. Heb. 13:6; Psa. 33:20.

        2. Satan is our hinderer. 1 Thess. 2:18.

            a. May use men as agents. Mt. 23:13; Lk. 11:52.

    B. Respecting What May We Be Hindered?

        1. The promulgation of the gospel. 1 Cor. 9:12.

        2. Our obedience to the truth. Gal. 5:7.

        3. Our prayers may be hindered. 1 Pet. 3:7; Cf. Mt. 5:23, 24.

        4. Our efforts to gain heaven. Lk. 13:24.

    C. Some Hindering Causes.

        1. Temptation. Lk. 8:13; 2 Pet. 3:17.

            a. This a varied cause - may cover every phase of hindrances.

            b. Should have whole armor to be able to stand. Eph. 6:11.

        2. Persecution. Mt. 13:21.

            a. Some cannot endure persecution. Mt. 24:12, 13.

            b. Paul took pleasure in persecution. 2 Cor. 12:10.

            c. When persecuted, should consider Christ. Heb.

12:3, 4.
3. Cares of this world. Mt. 13:22.
   a. Anxiety over crop failures, etc. cools our zeal.
   b. Should cast our cares upon God. 1 Pet. 5:7; Phil.
      4:6.
4. Pleasures of life. Lk. 8:14.
   a. A great hindrance to Christianity today. Cf. 2
      Tim. 3:4.
   b. Solomon pronounced them vanity. Eccl. 2:1-11.
5. False teachers. Lk. 11:52.
   a. This was the trouble at Galatia. Gal. 1:6, 7.
   b. Must know the truth and stand for it. 1 Jno. 4:1;
      Jude 3.
6. Popularity. Jno. 12:42, 43.
   a. No sin to receive the favor of men. Acts 2:47.
   b. Must not make it our aim. Lk. 16:15; Gai. 1:10.
7. Indifference. Heb. 2:3.
   a. Should not become slothful. Rom. 12:11.
   b. Lukewarmness the worst state possible. Rev.
      3:15-17.
8. Unbelief. Heb. 3:18, 19.
   a. The great sin of 20th century - infidelity in
      schools.
   b. This greatest hindrance facing the gospel today.
9. Ignorance. 1 Cor. 8:7.
   a. Study and teaching required to overcome it. 2
      Tim. 2:15; 2:2.
10. Weakness. 1 Cor. 8;11; Cf. Rom. 14:1.
   a. Failure to commemorate death of Christ pro-
      duces weakness. 1 Cor. 11:30.

III. Conclusion.
   A. We can overcome hindrances if we will.
   B. Cannot afford to be hindered.
   C. If God is for us, who against us. Rom. 9:31.

The Great Invitation
Mt. 11:28

I. **Introduction.**
   A. Invitations appreciated when offered in sincerity.
   B. A benediction in very sound of words of text.
   C. Myriads of human souls have been comforted by them.
   D. They are more impressive when we observe the setting.

II. **Discussion.**
   A. Setting of The Text.
      1. Till now his work unbroken success - so great, shared it with the 12.
      2. Turning point on 11th chapter - all his acts might be headed - "offence."
         a. John became doubtful of his divinity. Mt. 11:2-6.
         b. Jews compared with children - neither pleased by wedding or funeral. Mt. 11:16-19.
         c. Then the woes of v. 20-24 - responsibility gauged by light.
      3. His divinity shown.
         a. Man would say. "I'm done with you" - Christ said, "come."
         b. Never read of any man saying, "come unto me."
   B. To Whom Addressed?
      1. Not to the irresponsible - infants or idiots.
      2. But to all the weary and heavy laden.
         a. People laden with ceremonies of law. Gal. 3:10; Mt. 23:2-4.
         b. Sinners wearied with slavery of sin. Prov. 13:15; Jno. 8:34; 2 Tim. 2:25, 26.
         c. Penitents burdened with the guilt of crime. Acts 2:37; 9:9; Cf. Rom. 7:13.
   C. Why Away?
      1. Not born away - explain. Psa. 51:4, 5.
      2. Each shall bear his own sin. Ezek. 18:2, 3, 20.

3. Away as result of "going astray." Isa. 53:6; 59:2, 3.

D. Those Invited Have Power To Come.
   1. Picture child tied to tree, father inviting to come get present.
   2. A mild picture compared to sinner, if totally depraved.
   3. No burden so heavy that we must keep it.
   4. The matter rests with our will. Lk. 13:34; Jno. 5:40; Rev. 22:17.

E. What It Means To Come To Christ.
   1. Not merely into his presence - many came in that sense. Mt. 22:16-40.
   2. May be among his worshippers, yet never come to him.
   3. It means to follow his teaching. Mt. 11:29; 9:9; Lk. 9:23; 14:33; 6:46.

F. The Offered Rest.
   1. A present rest in Christ. Rom. 5:1; 2 Thess. 3:16.
      a. A rest from the rites of the law. Rom. 10:4. Acts 15:10; Gal. 5:4.
      b. A rest from the bondage of sin. Jno. 8:36; Rom. 6:17-18.
      c. A rest from the guilt of sin. Acts 8:39; 9:19; 16:34.
   2. A future rest beyond. Heb. 4:9-11; Psa. 55:6.
      a. A rest from all outward afflictions. Rev. 21:4.
      b. A rest from our labors. Rev. 14:13; Heb. 4:10.
      c. A rest Satan's temptations. Jas. 1:12; 1 Pet. 1:6.
      d. A rest from wickedness of others. Job 3:17; Cf. 2 Pet. 2:7, 8.
      e. A rest from all sin. 2 Pet. 3:13; Rev. 21:27.
      f. A rest from unsatisfied desires. Psa. 17:15; 1 Jno. 3:2.

G. How Come To Christ?
   1. Must submit to God's drawing power. Jno. 6:44, 45.
   2. Meet the terms in God's plan. Rom. 10:9, 10; Acts 11:18; Gal. 3:27.
   3. Final rest conditioned on faithfulness. Heb. 3:18, 19; 4:11.

III. Conclusion.
A. His rest is a glorious rest. Isa. 11:10.
B. Will not reject those who come. Jno. 6:37.
C. Let all the restless come and find rest.

www.ingramcontent.com/pod-product-compliance
Lightning Source LLC
Chambersburg PA
CBHW032053080426
42733CB00006B/255